Study Guide

for

Bardes, Shelley, and Schmidt's

American Government and Politics Today: The Essentials

2006-2007 Edition

Lisa Langenbach
Middle Tennessee State University

THOMSON

WADSWORTH

Australia • Brazil • Canada • Mexico • Singapore • Spain • United Kingdom • United States

Printed in the United States of America

1 2 3 4 5 6 7 09 08 07 06 05

Printer: Thomson West

ISBN 0-534-63190-8

Thomson Higher Education
10 Davis Drive
Belmont, CA 94002-3098
USA

For more information about our products, contact us at:
Thomson Learning Academic Resource Center
1-800-423-0563

For permission to use material from this text or product, submit a request online at
http://www.thomsonrights.com.
Any additional questions about permissions can be submitted by email to **thomsonrights@thomson.com.**

Contents

Preface

This Study Guide is part of a comprehensive instructional package designed to accompany *American Government and Politics Today: The Essentials, 2006-2007 edition.* The purpose of this guide is to aid you in using the instructional package in the most effective and time efficient manner. The Study Guide will highlight the key features that the authors have incorporated in the text, to facilitate your mastery of the concepts involved, as well as, provide information about resources available on the Internet to enhance your study efforts. This total package should allow you to successfully complete your course in American government.

The Preface to the text gives an overview of the Special Pedagogical Aids and High-Interest Features, which will allow mastery of the key concepts of American Government in conjunction with the use of the Study Guide. I would suggest that you read over this section of the text very carefully before beginning to read and study Chapter 1.

The Study Guide will provide an annotated topical outline to allow you to gain an overview of the important concepts presented in each chapter of the text. Following the outline will be a focus on margin definitions of key terms, which can be used to begin to assemble an understanding of the important concepts.

Exam questions will allow you to analyze your level of understanding of important concepts. The Study Guide will contain both subjective and objective questions. The short essay subjective questions can be written in each chapter of the Guide to provide an opportunity to think about and process the concepts and prepare you for these types of questions on examinations. The objective questions include fill-in-the-blank, true/false, and multiple choice. Answers to the questions are provided at the end of each chapter.

A companion Web site is available at http://politicalscience.wadsworth.com/bardes_essentials12/ to provide additional support in an interactive format. This will facilitate answering questions in a more realistic examination setting, and you will receive rapid feedback on your mastery of the concepts.

I hope that you find this Guide useful in maximizing your time and effort to learn the complexities of American Government and Politics. I wish you success in your endeavors, as it seems our country needs more than ever to increase the number of informed citizens who will take an active role in the democratic process.

Chapter 1
THE DEMOCRATIC REPUBLIC

CHAPTER SUMMARY

For many people, politics is a great game—better than soccer, better than chess. And this game is played for high stakes. Politics can affect not only your wallet but also what you do in your spare time and even your entire life. This chapter will discuss some of the questions and principles that are fundamental to the American, and any political system.

Politics and Government

Politics is defined by Harold Lasswell as "Who get what, when, and how?" in a society. The authors of the text define politics as the reference to conflict and conflict resolution in society. Conflict is always present in society for three major reasons. One, the differences of belief or ideology. Two, the differences in the perceived goals of the society. Three, scarce resources exist, and not every want can be satisfied by society. By necessity, the government spending more on senior citizens will mean spending less on younger people.

Why is Government Necessary?

Government refers to the institutions by which conflicts are resolved and values allocated. These institutions require authority, legitimacy, and power in order to accomplish their purpose to resolve conflict. Authority is the feature of a leader or institution that compels obedience. Usually this obedience is become of legitimacy. Legitimacy is the status conferred by the people on the officials, acts, and institutions of the government. The people believe the actions taken are legal and right. Power is the ability to cause others to modify their behavior and to conform to what the power holder wants. To sum up, authority is the legal use of power.

Democracy and Other Forms of Government

There is a variety of different types of government that can be classified according to which person or group of people controls society through the government. This section discusses totalitarian regimes, authoritarianism, autocracy, theocracy, and different types of democracy.

What Kind of Democracy Do We Have?

A fundamental question of politics has to with who makes political decisions for a society. Anarchy is the state in which no government exists, and individuals must try to resolve conflicts on their own. In an Oligarchy, a few members of the elite make decisions. An elite is defined as a member of an upper socioeconomic class. Aristocracy refers to decisions made by the best suited in terms of wealth, education, intelligence, and family prestige. In a Democracy, the majority of people make decisions. Direct Democracy is where people make decisions in person, like the New England town meeting. A possible danger of this form democracy can be mob rule, in which the majority abuses the rights of minority groups. This danger has led our society to create a Republic or representative Democracy, in which representatives are elected by the people to make and enforce laws. The three principles essential for democratic government in our society are universal suffrage, the right of all adults to vote for representatives; majority rule with the protection of minority rights; and limited government, the authority of government is limited by a written document or widely held beliefs.

Elite theory has suggested that society is ruled by a small number of wealthy people who exercise power in their self-interest. The primary goal of such a society is stability because elites do not want to see any change in their status. Pluralism theory has proposed that conflict in society is among interest groups. Bargaining and compromise among groups determine political decision-making. Hyperpluralism has suggested that interest groups can become so powerful that the society is virtually paralyzed by the struggle between interest groups.

Fundamental Values

Political Culture can be defined as a patterned set of ideas, values, and ways of thinking about government and politics. The process by which such beliefs and values are transmitted to Immigrants and our children is called Political Socialization.

The Fundamental Values of the American political culture can be defined as: liberty, the greatest freedom of individuals that is consistent with the freedom of other individuals in society; equality, all people are of equal worth; and property, the right of individual ownership. Political culture has been important in holding society together by persuading people to support the existing political process. The disputed 2000 presidential election showed the stability of the American political culture, as only 17 percent of Americans polled ever described the situations as a crisis.

Ideas and Politics: Ideology

Ideology can be defined as a comprehensive and logical set of beliefs about the nature of people and about the institutions and role of government. American ideology has been dominated by two moderate ideologies. Liberalism is the belief that includes support of positive government action to improve the welfare of individuals, support of civil rights, and the call for political and social change. Conservatism is the belief that includes support of a limited role for government helping individuals, support for traditional values, and a cautious response to change.

The Changing Face of America

The context of the American society is changing as Americans age, become more diverse, and need new laws and policies. Almost 13% of the population was sixty-five years or older in 2000. Combined with low birth rates, this has important implications for retirement and pension systems, including Social Security. The shrinking of the younger population is a worldwide event in developed countries. Hispanics, African Americans, and Asian Americans have become a larger proportion of the United States population because of higher birth rates and immigration increases. Other trends reveal that over 75% of the population lived in urban areas in 2002. Today, 25% of children live in one-parent households. National surveys have found about 20% of all Americans are barely literate.

America's Politics: Why Is it Important Today?

Today, what happens in government at all levels is more important than at any time since World War II. In these troubled times, citizens must be better informed and must increase their level of participation in the political process. The discussion of how serious the political situation is has produced debate about requiring voters to pass a test before being able to vote.

KEY TERMS

Aristocracy — p. 5
Authoritarianism — p. 5
authority — p. 5
capitalism — p. 14
communism — p. 18
consent of the people — p. 7
conservatism — p. 15
democracy — p. 5
democratic republic — p. 8
direct democracy — p. 6
dominant culture — p. 11
elite theory — p. 9
equality — p. 12
fascism — p. 18
government — p. 3
Hispanic — p. 21
ideology — p. 14
initiative — p. 7

institution — p. 3
legislature — p. 6
legitimacy — p. 5
liberalism — p. 15
libertarianism — p. 16
liberty — p. 5
limited government — p. 9
majoritarianism — p. 9
majority — p. 8
majority rule — p. 8
order — p. 3
pluralism — p. 10
political culture — p. 10
political socialization — p. 10
politics — p. 3
popular sovereignty — p. 7
property — p. 14
recall — p. 7

referendum — p. 7
representative democracy — p. 8
republic — p. 7
socialism — p. 16

theocracy — p. 5
totalitarian regime — p. 5
universal suffrage — p. 8

PRACTICE EXAM
(Answers appear at the end of this chapter.)

Fill-In-The-Blank Supply the missing word(s) or term to complete the sentence.

1. The greatest freedom of individuals that is consistent with the freedom of other individuals in the society is called _liberty_.

2. The feature of a leader or an institution that compels obedience is called _authority_

3. The ancient Greek city-state of Athens is often considered to be the historical model for _direct democracy_

4. The U.S. Constitution creates a form of republican government known as a _representative democracy_

5. From the elite theory perspective, the primary goal of government is _____, because elites do not want any change to their status.

6. In the pluralist's view, politics is the struggle among _____ to gain benefits for their members.

7. A form of government that controls all aspects of the political and social life of a nation is referred to as a _totalitarian regime_.

8. In a _theocracy_, the governing principles are rooted in religious precepts—there is no separation of church and state.

9. A theory that views politics as a conflict among interest groups and in which political decision making is characterized by bargaining and compromise is known as _pluralism_.

10. Within the American electorate, the two ideological viewpoints that are most commonly held are _liberalism_ and _conservatism_

11. The _dominant culture_ of a nation are the group or groups that have traditionally controlled politics and government in that society.

12. A set of beliefs that includes a limited role for the national government in helping individuals, support for traditional values and lifestyles, and a cautious response to change is called _conservatism_

True/False. Circle the appropriate letter to indicate if the statement is true or false.

(T)   F   1. A political ideology is a comprehensive set of beliefs about politics.

(T)   F   2. In democratic nations, most citizens comply with the law because they accept the authority of the government and its officials.

(T)   F   3. Direct democracy in ancient Athens was considered to have been the ideal form of democracy.

T   (F)   4. James Madison was a strong advocate of a "pure democracy" for the American political system.

(T)   F   5. In a representative democracy, the people hold the ultimate power over the government through the election process.

T   (F)   6. The elite perspective sees the mass population as active and involved in the decisions of government.

T   F   7. A set of beliefs that includes the advocacy of positive government action to improve the welfare of individuals, support for civil rights, and tolerance for political and social change is known as _____.

T   F   8. When there is no regulation of the economy, we call that conservatism.

T   F   9. Fascism is often a totalitarian ideology.

T   F   10. In recent years, the United States has experienced falling birth rates and an increase in the number of older citizens.

Multiple Choice. Circle the correct response.

1. The idea that all people are of equal worth is called
    a. fairness.
    b. equanimity.
    c. equality.
    d. socialism.

2. A form of government in which every aspect of political, social, and economic life is controlled by the government is called a(n)
    a. Democratic regime.
    b. Socialist regime.
    c. Totalitarian regime.
    d. Oligarchy.

3. This political ideology champions elite values, action over rational deliberation, rejects liberal individualism, and exalts patriotism and nationalism. It is called
    a. communism.
    b. Republicanism.
    c. libertarianism.
    d. fascism.

4. The Athenian model of government was considered
    a. the ideal form of direct democracy.
    b. a weak and ineffective form of government.
    c. the reason the Roman legions were able to conquer Greece.
    d. the forerunner of communism.

5. Initiative is a procedure by which voters can
    a. directly make laws.
    b. remove elected officials.
    c. propose a law or constitutional amendment.
    d. place candidates on a ballot.

6. The U.S. Constitution creates a form of republican government known as a
    a. pure democracy.
    b. confederation.
    c. representative democracy.
    d. majoritarian system.

7. A central feature to the American governmental system is
    a. the supremacy of Congress over the other branches.
    b. control of the airwaves.
    c. the tendency to provide foreign aid to every country.
    d. equality of every individual before the law.

8. To ensure that majority rule does not become oppressive, modern democracies
   a. provide guarantees of minority rights.
   b. have constitutions that are difficult to amend.
   c. use plurality voting for most decisions.
   d. hold free, competitive elections.

9. By 2050, the U.S. is expected to have a population close to _____ million.
   a. 250
   b. 360
   c. 420
   d. 510

10. The average number of children a group of women are expected to have over the course of a lifetime is called the
    a. fertility rate.
    b. birth rate.
    c. rate of change.
    d. lifetime reproduction rate.

11. Pluralist theory believes that decisions are made in American politics by
    a. the mass population.
    b. the governing elites.
    c. the wealthy.
    d. the competition between groups trying to gain benefits for their members.

12. The fastest growing minority in the US are
    a. African-Americans.
    b. Muslims.
    c. Asian-Americans.
    d. Hispanics.

13. The pattern of political beliefs and values characteristics of a community or population is referred to as
    a. public opinion.
    b. democratic heritage.
    c. political culture.
    d. consensus of opinion.

14. The process by which Americans come to accept a single set of values concerning the Political system is called
    a. enculturation.
    b. education.
    c. political socialization.
    d. propaganda.

15. Democracy, liberty, equality, and property are
    a. concepts that no longer have meaning in modern political systems.
    b. now thought to be unattainable in a modern pluralistic society.
    c. concepts that lie at the core of American political culture.
    d. concepts that encompass our entire political heritage.

16. The ideology that believes the government should exercise the least power is
    a. Socialism.
    b. Liberalism.
    c. Conservatism.
    d. Libertarianism.

17. Most immigrants to the US come from
    a. India.
    b. Mexico.
    c. Africa.
    d. South America.

18. The loss of property without compensation is referred to as
    a. violent property right.
    b. forfeiture.
    c. communism.
    d. seizure.

19. A type of government in which there is no separation of church and state and in which governing principles are rooted in religious precepts is called
    a. fascism.
    b. theocracy.
    c. democracy.
    d. authoritarianism.

20. The idea that government and laws derive their legitimacy from the consent of the governed is called
    a. republicanism.
    b. popular sovereignty.
    c. consent of the governed.
    d. democracy.

Short Essay Questions. Briefly address the major concepts raised by the following questions.

1. Explain the role of politics in an organized society.

2. Explain the origins of democracy and the different types of democracy.

3. Define the fundamental elements of the American political culture.

4. Compare and contrast the concepts of liberalism and conservatism.

ANSWERS TO THE PRACTICE EXAM

Fill-in-the-Blank

1. liberty
2. Authority
3. Direct democracy
4. Representative democracy
5. totalitarian regime
6. theocracy
7. pluralism
8. political culture
9. dominant culture
10. Conservatism

True/False.

1. T	3. T	5. T	7. T	9. F
2. T	4. F	6. F	8. F	10. T

Multiple Choice.

1. c	6. c	11. d	16. c
2. c	7. d	12. d	17. b
3. d	8. a	13. c	18. b
4. a	9. c	14. c	19. b
5. c	10. a	15. c	20. c

Short Essay.

An adequate short answer consists of several paragraphs that relate to concepts addressed by the question. Always demonstrate your knowledge of the ideas by giving examples. The following represent major ideas that should be included in the short essay answer.

1.   Explain the role of politics in an organized society.
   - Definitions of politics—Harold Lasswell, and your author's
   - Government and power
   - Authority and Legitimacy

2.   Explain the origins of democracy and the different types of democracy.
   - Athenian model of direct democracy—Every citizen has a responsibility to participate through initiative, referendum, and recall.
   - Representative democracy—a Republic in which the people vote for representatives to make laws and other decisions for the people.
   - Principles of western representative democracy—the emphasis on elected officials making all policy decisions.
   - Constitutional democracy—Limited government, that is the power of government is limited by a written document or constitution.

3.   Define the fundamental values of the American political culture.
   Liberty—The greatest freedom of individuals that is consistent with the freedom of other individuals in society. Freedom of speech and freedom of religion are good examples.
   Equality—A concept that all people are of equal worth. This concept is often debated as to its meaning. Does it mean equal political status or equal opportunity? Perhaps the Internet will provide persons with a forum in which all are equal
   Property—can be seen as giving its owner political power and the liberty to do whatever he or she wants. These are the three core values often linked with majority rule.

4.   Compare and contrast the concepts of liberalism and conservatism.
   - Ideology—a set of ideas about the goal of politics
     - Liberals
     - Positive government action to solve social problems
     - Advocates for civil rights
     - Advocates for social change

     - Conservatives
     - Faith in the private sector to solve most social problems
     - Advocates for individual action to protect rights
     - Advocates for a return to traditional values

Chapter 2
THE CONSTITUTION

CHAPTER SUMMARY

The story of the creation of the constitution is told in each generation and is the key to understanding American Government and Politics.

Initial Colonizing Efforts

The first British settlement in North American was Roanoke Island, which mysteriously disappeared. Recent research has indicated that a severe drought must have wiped out the colony. Jamestown, Virginia and Plymouth, Massachusetts, in 1607 and 1620 respectively, were the first successful settlements. Additional settlements followed in Massachusetts and Connecticut.

British Restrictions and Colonial Grievances

The British government decided to tax the colonists to pay for French and Indian War expenses. The Sugar Act in 1764 and Stamp Act in 1765 led to the Boston Tea Party, which caused the British Parliament to pass The Coercive or (Intolerable) Acts in 1774.

The Colonial Response: The Continental Congresses

The colonists responded to the British by the **First Continental Congress** held in 1774, which issued a petition of grievances and attempted to create committees to bring the colonists together. The **Second Continental Congress** met in 1775, at which point fighting had already occurred between the colonists and the British. The Second Congress established an army with George Washington as commander in chief.

Declaring Independence

In early 1776, the Second Continental Congress approved the **Resolution of Independence** to establish legitimacy and to seek foreign military aid. The Second Congress assigned Thomas Jefferson the task of writing a formal declaration of independence. This **Declaration of Independence** was approved on July 4, 1776 and contained three major principles, based on the ideas of English political philosopher John Locke. These concepts were natural rights, consent of the governed, and the right to change the government.

The Rise of Republicanism

Colonists, who called themselves Republicans, were opposed to any strong central government. They were a powerful political force in the creation of strong state government in the 1776 to 1780 time period.

The Articles of Confederation: Our First Form of Government

In 1781, the Articles of Confederation, a voluntary association of independent states, were created. [See Figure 2-1 and Table 2-1 for information on powers of this form of government.] The lack of taxing authority made the Articles too weak a form of government to survive. Shay's Rebellion in 1786 spurred political leaders to take action to change the Articles.

Drafting the Constitution

The Annapolis Convention was called in 1786 to discuss the weaknesses of the nation. At this meeting, a call was sent out for all of the states to attend a general convention in Philadelphia in May 1787. 55 delegates from every state except Rhode Island attended the Philadelphia convention. The delegates were mostly nationalists but included monarchists, democratic nationalists, non-democratic nationalists, and some strong state government advocates.

The debates, which began the first day, produced two major plans: The **Virginia Plan**, which proposed an entirely new national government, favoring big states, and the **New Jersey Plan**, which was an amendment to the Articles of Confederation. The "Great Compromise," brokered by the Connecticut delegation, broke the deadlock between these two proposals. This compromise called for a **bicameral legislature** as a new form of national government. Slavery and other issues between the agrarian South and the mercantile North were resolved by other compromises, including the Three-Fifths Compromise. The final agreement included **separation of powers** (sometimes known as the **Madisonian model**), a system of **checks and balances**, and an **electoral college** to elect the president. [See Figure 2-2 for a view of the check and balance system.]

The Final Document

Thirty-nine delegates approved the Constitution on September 17, 1787. The document established five fundamental principles: 1. Popular sovereignty, 2. A republican form of government, 3. Limited government, 4. Separation of powers, and 5. A federal system.

The Difficult Road to Ratification

The opposing forces in the battle for ratification were the **Federalists**, in favor of ratification, and the **Anti-Federalists**, who were opposed to ratifying the Constitution as it was drafted. Hamilton, Madison, and Jay, wrote the Federalists Papers, which were influential in the success of the ratification effort.

In 1788, the ninth state, New Hampshire, ratified the Constitution, to formally establish it.

The Bill of Rights

Ratification of the Constitution was probably dependent on the Federalists promises of amendments to the Constitution to protect individual liberties. James Madison culled through state convention recommendations to produce what became the Bill of Rights. One of the amendments proposed was not ratified until 1992, when it became the 27th amendment to the constitution. The 10 amendments of the Bill of Rights were ratified in 1791.

Altering the Constitution: The Formal Amendment Process

Amending the constitution is a two-step process. The first step is proposing a new amendment. This can be done by either a two-thirds vote in both houses of Congress or by a national convention called by Congress at the request of two-thirds of the states. The second step in amending the constitution is to ratify the amendment. Ratification can be done by either a three-fourths vote of the state legislatures or by a three-fourths vote of state conventions called to ratify the amendment. Congress has considered more than 11,000 amendments, of which 33 have been submitted for ratification, and only 27 have been ratified. [See Table 2-3.] Since 1919, most proposed amendments have had a seven-year ratification limit, but the 27th amendment ratified in 1992 took 203 years.

Informal Methods of Constitutional Change

While there have few formal amendments to the constitution over the centuries, informal change has occurred on a more frequent basis. These informal changes have been by legislation passed by Congress under the commerce clause and Article III, Section 1 of the constitution. The constitution has changed by the creation of executive agreements by Presidents to conduct foreign policy. The Supreme Court has claimed the power of judicial review in the case of Marbury v. Madison (1803). Finally, through the usage in day-to-day government activities, interpretation, custom, and tradition have influenced the meaning of the constitution.

The Constitution: Why Is It Important Today?

The U.S. constitution is the longest-lived written constitution and most imitated in the world. We must not take our constitution for granted. As Benjamin Franklin said about the kind of government created by the constitution, it is "A republic, if you can keep it". We must support the reality of the constitutional concepts and insist that our government enforce those concepts.

KEY TERMS

Anti-federalist — p. 47
bicameral legislature — p. 41
checks and balances — p. 44
confederation — p. 36
electoral college — p. 45

executive agreement — p. 55
federal system — p.46
Federalist — p. 47
Great Compromise — p. 41
judicial review — p. 55

Madisonian model — p. 44
natural rights — p. 35
ratification — p. 46
representative assembly — p. 31
separation of powers — p. 44

social contract — p.36
state — p. 36
supremacy doctrine — p. 41
unicameral legislature — p. 36

PRACTICE EXAM

(Answers appear at the end of this chapter.)

Fill-in-the-Blank.   Supply the missing word(s) or term to complete the sentence.

1. The passage of the Coercive Acts by the British Parliament was in response to the *Boston Tea Party*

2. The rights of "life, liberty, and the pursuit of happiness" are referred to as *Natural rights* .

3. A voluntary association of independent states is referred to as *Confederation* .

4. The plan of government that introduced the idea of a bicameral legislature was the *Virginia Plan* .

5. The agreement that resolved the differences between the large and small states over representation in the new government was the *Great Compromise* .

6. Nowhere in the *Constitution* are the words slavery or slaves used.

7. *Federalists* was the name given to those who favored the adoption of the new constitution.

8. The *Federalists Papers* are considered by many to be the best example of political theorizing ever produced in the United States.

9. The *27th Amendment* was one of the two "lost" amendments of the twelve bill of rights amendments that originally went to the states in 1789.

10. The *Supreme Court* is the only court specially created in the Constitution.

True/False.   Circle the appropriate letter to indicate if the statement is true or false.

(T)   F   1. The Mayflower Compact embodied the idea of majority rule as a theory of government.

(T)   F   2. Thomas Paine's pamphlet *Common Sense* popularized the idea of independence from Great Britain.

T   (F)   3. According to the Declaration of Independence, these United Colonies are, and of right ought to be free and independent states.

(T)   F   4. The most fundamental weakness of the Articles of Confederation was the inability of the Congress to raise money for the militia.

(T)   F   5. A majority of delegates to the Constitutional convention were in favor of a stronger central government.

T   (F)   6. The Virginia plan called for each state to have equal representation in the new government.

T   (F)   7. The Anti-federalists believed that the central government should be strengthened over the states because the states were apt to abuse personal liberties.

T   (F)   8. The delegates to the Constitution Convention represented a good cross-section of eighteenth-century American society.

T   (F)   9. The only way to formally amend the Constitution is by a 4/5 vote of all of the state legislatures.

(T)   F   10. An informal way to amend the Constitution is by judicial review.

Multiple Choice. Circle the correct response.

1. "Starving time for Virginia" may have been caused by:
    a. Indian hostilities.
    b. British reluctance to feed the colony.
    c. a severe drought.
    d. massive British taxes.

2. The last of the thirteen colonies to be established was
    a. Rhode Island.
    b. Connecticut.
    c. New Hampshire.
    d. Georgia.

3. The British government imposed taxes on the American colonies to pay for
    a. war with Spain.
    b. the costs of westward expansion of colonies.
    c. the costs of the French and Indian War.
    d. the costs of exploring India.

4. Thomas Paine's pamphlet *Common Sense*
    a. called for a cessation of hostilities against the British.
    b. pointed out in "common sense" terms why America should break with Britain.
    c. was a propaganda tool used by the British to gain popular consent to their governing of the colonies.
    d. apparently had very little effect on popular opinion about the revolution.

5. One of the revolutionary ideas of John Locke was the idea that people have
    a. a right to a secure job.
    b. a right to welfare if they need it.
    c. natural rights.
    d. a right to checks and balances in government.

6. During the Revolutionary War, the creation of state governments was strongly influenced by groups calling themselves
    a. Federalists.
    b. Democrats.
    c. Republicans.
    d. Monarchists.

7. The government under the Articles of Confederation Congress included a
    a. president, but no congress.
    b. congress and a president.
    c. unicameral legislature.
    d. strong central government.

8. Under the Articles of Confederation,
    a. each state had one vote.
    b. the national courts were the supreme authority.
    c. the congress imposed heavy taxes.
    d. the president ultimately controlled the government.

9.   An important accomplishment of the Articles of Confederation was
     a.   the creation of a common currency.
     b.   settling states' claims to western lands.
     c.   the creation of national tax collections.
     d.   the creation of a strong national army.

10. Under the Article of Confederation, the Congress had the power to
     a.   declare war and make peace.
     b.   draft soldiers into military service.
     c.   compel states to pay their share of national government costs.
     d.   regulate interstate and foreign commerce.

11. Shay's rebellion demonstrated that the central government
     a.   had the capability to protect citizens from riots and civil unrest.
     b.   could not protect the citizenry from armed rebellion.
     c.   dared not confront state militias.
     d.   could easily incite citizens to riot.

12. The only state that refused to send delegates to the Constitution Convention was
     a.   New Hampshire.
     b.   Rhode Island.
     c.   New York.
     d.   Virginia.

13. The proceedings in the Constitutional Convention were kept secret because
     a.   the delegates were doing something illegal.
     b.   the public would not understand the issues involved and would create confusion.
     c.   all meetings of this nature must be secret.
     d.   if the proceeding were public, the delegates might have a more difficult time compromising on issues.

14. The Great Compromise
     a.   resulted in the Bill of Rights being added to the Constitution.
     b.   broke the deadlock between the large and small states over the nature of representation in the new national government.
     c.   established the Electoral College as the vehicle for electing the president.
     d.   allowed George Washington to be nominated and elected the first president.

15. The Madisonian Model of a government scheme refers to
     a.   direct democracy.
     b.   judicial review.
     c.   a separation of powers.
     d.   the supremacy of national laws over state laws.

16. The power of judicial review comes from
     a.   the Constitution.
     b.   the Bill of Rights.
     c.   the case of *Marbury v. Madison*.
     d.   executive agreements.

17. Which of the following are ways to amend the Constitution?
     a.   a majority vote of citizens
     b.   a majority vote of Congress
     c.   a two-thirds vote of Congress
     d.   judicial review by the Supreme Court

18. The Federalists Papers were
    a. largely written by Thomas Jefferson.
    b. so brilliant the Anti-Federalists could not respond.
    c. not very significant as political theory.
    d. responded to by Anti-Federalist political theory.

19. The leading political figure responsible for recommending the Bill of Rights was
    a. Jefferson.
    b. Madison.
    c. Washington.
    d. Franklin.

20. Which of the following was not mentioned in the Constitution?
    a. the electoral college
    b. the Supreme Court
    c. political parties
    d. a national convention to propose constitutional amendments

Short Essay Questions. Briefly address the major concepts raised by the following questions.

1. Identify the milestone political documents that moved the colonies from the Mayflower Compact to the Constitutional Convention.

2. Trace the events and circumstances that led to the Revolutionary War.

3. Summarize the events leading to the call for a Constitutional Convention.

4. Explain the compromises over the organization of the government designed by the delegates to the Constitutional Convention.

ANSWERS TO THE PRACTICE EXAM

Fill-in-the-Blank.

1. Boston Tea Party
2. Natural rights
3. Confederation
4. Virginia Plan
5. Great Compromise
6. Constitution
7. Federalists
8. Federalists Papers
9. 27th Amendment
10. Supreme Court

True/False.

1. T	3. F	5. T	7. F	9. F
2. T	4. T	6. F	8. F	10. T

Multiple Choice.

1. c	6. c	11. b	16. c
2. d	7. c	12. b	17. d
3. c	8. a	13. d	18. d
4. b	9. b	14. b	19. b
5. c	10. a	15. c	20. c

Short Essay.

An adequate short answer consists of several paragraphs that relate to concepts addressed by the question. Always demonstrate your knowledge of the ideas by giving examples. The following represent major ideas that should be included in the short essay answer.

1. Identify the milestone political documents that moved the colonies from the Mayflower Compact to the Constitutional Convention.

   - Refer to the timeline on page 32 to give you a good overview of the question.
   - The Mayflower Compact of 1620 was a political agreement derived from the consent of the people.
   - The Fundamental Orders of Connecticut, 1639, was the first written constitution.
   - The Massachusetts Body of Liberties, 1641, was the first constitution to include protection of individual rights.
   - The Pennsylvania Charter of Privileges, 1701, contained a constitution and bill of rights and offered a precedent and rationale for our national Constitution.
   - The Declaration of Independence, 1776, advocated independence from Great Britain.
   - The Articles of Confederation, 1781, described the first attempt at an independent national government based on a confederation.

2. Trace the events and circumstances that led to the Revolutionary War.

   - Address this question in chronological/historical order.
   - Explain the reasons for British restrictions represented by the Sugar Act, Stamp Act, and Coercive Act.
   - Describe the colonial response as seen in the First and Second Continental Congresses and Paine's *Common Sense.*
   - Describe the Resolution of Independence and Declaration of Independence.

3. Summarize the events that led to the call for the Constitutional Convention.

   - Explain the development of the Articles of Confederation structure and the distribution of power.
   - Explain the weaknesses of the Articles of Confederation as seen in the lack of good will among the states and the inability to tax for national needs.
   - Explain the impact of Shay's Rebellion

4. Explain the compromises that evolved at the Constitutional Convention and pertained to the organization of the government.

   - Discuss the various proposed structures for the new government as seen in the Virginia Plan and the New Jersey Plan
   - Describe the Great Compromise.
   - Discuss the distribution of governmental power as represented by Madison's theories of a separation of powers and a system of checks and balances.

Chapter 3
FEDERALISM

CHAPTER SUMMARY
Government in the United States consists of one national government, fifty state governments, and so many local governments to create a grand total of more than 87,900. [See Table 3-1.]

Three Systems of Government
There are basically three ways of organizing governmental structures. [See Figure 3-1 for flow of power in the three systems.] A Unitary system allows ultimate governmental authority in the national government. A Confederate system is a league of independent states. A Federal system divides government authority between a national government and state government.

Why Federalism?
The United State developed a federal system because it was a practical solution that retained state traditions and local power while it created a strong national government. Federalism also solved the problem of geographical size and regional isolation. Other arguments for federalism were it diffused political dissatisfaction among the different governments, provided a training ground for future national leaders, allowed diverse groups to develop in their own regions, and brought government closer to the people. Certainly not every political viewpoint supported federalism. Some of the arguments against federalism were it provided a way for powerful state and local interests to block national progress, allowed for the possibility of expansion of national powers at the expense of states, and provided a way for powerful state and local interests to deny equal rights for minorities.

The Constitutional Basis for American Federalism
While the Constitution does not directly refer to federalism, it does divide government power into national government, state government, and powers prohibited to government. National government power can be described as enumerated, implied, and inherent. Enumerated powers are found in the first seventeen clauses of Article I, Section 8. Implied powers come from the necessary and proper clause, the last clause of Article I, Section 8. Inherent powers come from the fact that governments have an inherent right to ensure their own survival. Powers given to state governments, called reserved powers, come from the 10th Amendment, which states that power, not enumerated or denied, is reserved to the states. A major state power is police power, which is the authority to legislate for the health, morals, safety, and welfare of the citizens of the states. National and state government shares some powers, like the power to tax. These shared powers are called concurrent powers. Powers denied to government are called prohibited powers and deny powers to both national and state governments. The supremacy clause, Article VI, Paragraph 2 provided that federal laws are superior to all conflicting state and local laws.

Defining Constitution Powers—The Early Years
To be effective over the centuries, the constitution had to be vague and flexible. Two vague areas that were subject to the interpretation of the Supreme Court were the necessary and proper and commerce clauses. In the case of **McCulloch v. Maryland (1819),** Chief Justice John Marshall ruled that the necessary and proper clause of Article I, Section 8 embraced all means that are appropriate to carry out the legitimate ends of the Constitution. In **Gibbons v. Ogden (1824),** Chief Justice Marshall ruled that the power to regulate interstate commerce in Article I, Section 8 was an exclusive national power.

States' Rights and the Resort to Civil War
The Jacksonian era (1829-1837) created a climate, in which most Southern states attempted to nullify national laws and to justify secession from the federal union. The defeat of the South in the Civil War ended the theory of nullification and secession. The war effort created a larger and more powerful national government, which for the first time imposed an income tax on its citizens.

The Continuing Dispute over the Division of Power

Although the outcome of the Civil War established the supremacy of the national government, the debate over the division of authority continued through the stages of dual federalism, cooperative federalism, and new federalism. In dual federalism, which faded in the 1930s, the state governments and national government are viewed as separate entities, like separate layers in a cake. Cooperative Federalism, which was created to deal with the disaster of the depression, advocated that the state governments and national government should cooperate in solving problems, like merged layers in a marble cake. In the 1960s, another metaphor for cooperative federalism developed called Picket-fence Federalism. This added local government to the federal mix, and was explained as the horizontal boards in the fence represent the national, state and local governments while the vertical pickets represent different programs and policies in which each level of government works to the develop the policy represented by the picket.

The key factors in understanding how these different types of federalism developed were Federal grants-in-aid. The three major types of federal grants are categorical grants-in-aid designed for very specific programs or projects of state and local governments; matching funds, which require state and local governments to put up a share of the money; and equalization funds, which take into account the relative wealth of the state or local entities. [See Figure 3-2 for each government spending.] Block Grants were developed under the administration of Ronald Reagan in 1980. These grants are federal programs that provide funding to state and local government for general functional areas with fewer restrictions than grants-in-aid. One major barrier to returning authority to state government is federal mandates. A federal mandate is a requirement in federal legislation that forces states and local governments to comply with certain rules.

The Politics of Federalism

The allocation of power between states and the national government has been and continues to be a controversial issue. Civil rights and the War on Poverty are examples of increasing national power to change society. Some states favor the status quo, with authority in a particular field, and yet there is great variation state to state.

Federalism and the Supreme Court

President George W. Bush emphasized this concept of Federalism, when he said "the people" should decide public policy for themselves at the state and local level. The tragic events of September 11, 2001 have hindered this position, as President George W. Bush has had to make important decisions at the national level of public policy. However, in the 1990s, the Supreme Court sought to limit national government power under the 10th amendment and the commerce clause. In the case of **United States v. Lopez** (1995) the Gun-Free School Zones Act of 1990, based on Congress power under the commerce clause, was ruled unconstitutional. In **Printz v. United States** (1997) provisions of the Brady Handgun violence Prevention Act of 1993, which required state employees to enforce these provisions, was ruled unconstitutional.

Federalism: Why Is It Important Today?

Our federal form of government means diversity because different state and local governments have different laws and policies. This can create conflict between states and between the state and national government. Some of these conflicts, which may be important to you, are discussed in these chapters. They include, educational standards, welfare payments, physician-assisted suicide, and the use of medical marijuana.

KEY TERMS

block grants — p. 98
categorical grants — p. 97
commerce clause — p. 91
concurrent powers — p. 86
confederal system — p. 82
cooperative federalism — p. 97
devolution — p. 102
dual federalism — p. 93
elastic clause/necessary and proper clause — p. 85

enumerated powers — p. 85
federal mandate — p. 99
interstate compact — p. 88
picket fence federalism — p. 97
police power — p. 86
supremacy clause — p. 87
unitary system — p. 82

PRACTICE EXAM
(Answers appear at the end of this chapter.)

Fill-in-the-Blank. Supply the missing word(s) or term to complete the sentence.

1. A system of government in which power is divided between a central and subdivision governments is called a ____federal____ system.

2. ____Inherent____ powers are those that are derived from the fact that the United States is a sovereign power among the nations.

3. The Tenth Amendment establishes the ____reserved____ powers to the states.

4. The denial of power to state and national government is referred to as ____prohibited____ ____powers____.

5. The legitimate exercise of national government power ____preempt____ any action by states.

6. The issue in the McCulloch v. Maryland case was whether the national government has ____implied____ powers.

7. President Reagan and Congressional Republicans supported the development of_____ grants.

8. The doctrine that emphasizes a distinction between federal and state spheres of governmental authority is referred to as _____ _____.

9. A major set of block grants related to state _____ programs.

10. ____Federal____ ____Mandates____ require state and local governments to comply with certain rules.

True/False. Circle the appropriate letter to indicate if the statement is true or false.

T̸ F   1. A unitary system of government is the easiest system to define.

T F̸   2. The United States Constitution expressly designates that we should have a federal system of government.

T F̸   3. The national government may deny the use of reserved powers to the states.

T̸ F   4. The Tenth Amendment provides for the reserved powers to the states.

T F̸   5. Most concurrent powers of the states are specifically stated in the Constitution.

T̸ F   6. The Civil War permanently ended the idea that any state can claim the right to secede.

T F̸   7. Chief Justice John Marshall was a strong supporter of state's rights.

T F̸   8. The case of McCulloch v. Maryland (1819) set a precedent for a narrow interpretation of the implied powers of Congress.

T̸ F   9. Dual federalism emphasizes a distinction between federal and state spheres of authority.

T̸ F   10. One way the national government has moderated the burden of federal mandates is by granting waivers.

Multiple Choice. Circle the correct response. The correct answers are at the end of the chapter.

1. The most popular way of ordering relations between central government and local units is by a
   a. Confederate system.
   b. Federal system.
   c. Unitary system.
   d. Constitutional system.

2. If ultimate governmental authority rests in the hands of a central government, that is a
   a. Federal system.
   b. Confederate system.
   c. Unitary system.
   d. Theocratic system.

3. A league of independent states, where the central government has only those matters expressly delegated to it, is a
   a. Federal system.
   b. Confederate system.
   c. Unitary system.
   d. Democratic system.

4. To the framers of the Constitution, the appeal of federalism was that it
   a. allowed the states to control the process of government decision-making.
   b. retained state traditions and local power while it established a strong national government.
   c. was acceptable to the British Parliament.
   d. did not change the status quo.

5. The essential argument in *Federalist Paper No. 10* is that
   a. a unitary government is the best kind of government for a diverse society.
   b. smaller political units are likely to be dominated by a single political group.
   c. a unitary system of government is the most efficient.
   d. only with a strong chief executive can the U.S. maintain its independence in world politics.

6. A special category of national powers that are not implied by the necessary and proper clause consists of those labeled as
   a. inherent powers.
   b. enumerated powers.
   c. extraordinary powers.
   d. elongated powers.

7. The constitutional concept of police powers is created by the
   a. 10th Amendment.
   b. necessary and proper clause.
   c. interstate commerce clause.
   d. combined power clause.

8. The issue in McCulloch v. Maryland was
   a. judiciary supremacy of the Supreme Court.
   b. the use of delegated power by the president.
   c. the commerce clause to regulate shipping on the open seas.
   d. the use of implied powers by the national government.

9. Grants to state and local governments designed for very specific programs and projects are referred to as
   a. block grants.
   b. revenue sharing.
   c. unfunded mandates.
   d. categorical grants-in-aid.

10. Picket-fence federalism refers to
    a. state and local governments.
    b. restoring more power to the national government.
    c. Congress.
    d. child labor laws.

11. Because of the supremacy clause the states cannot
     a. deny citizens of another state the same privileges and immunities they extend to their own citizens.
     b. use their reserved or concurrent powers to thwart national policies.
     c. discriminate against citizens from another state.
     d. tax their citizens beyond national governmental rates.

12. Picket-fence federalism added what element to the national and state governments?
     a. interest groups
     b. local government
     c. multi-national corporations
     d. political parties

13. In the cases of Printz v. U.S. and U.S. v. Lopez, the Supreme Court ruled that
     a. the national government exceeded its regulatory powers.
     b. the state government exceeded its reserved powers.
     c. the local government exceeded its police powers.
     d. both state and national government exceeded constitutional powers.

14. The concept of cooperative federalism was coined by political scientists after the administration of
     a. George Washington.
     b. Abraham Lincoln.
     c. Franklin D. Roosevelt.
     d. Ronald Reagan.

15. The case of United States v. Morrison dealt with the issue of
     a. Congress overreaching its authority.
     b. states overreaching their authority.
     c. private foundations overreaching their authority.
     d. multi-national corporations overreaching their authority.

16. Block grants are a tool that helped establish
     a. less restrictions on state and local governments.
     b. dual federalism.
     c. more strings on state and local governments.
     d. no difference in federalism.

17. Federal Mandates are
     a. programs funded by Congress.
     b. programs funded by states.
     c. programs not required to be funded.
     d. being phased out by Congress.

18. Which Supreme Court case involved an issue of the Eleventh Amendment?
     a. Marbury v. Madison
     b. U.S. v. Lopez
     c. U.S. v. Morrison
     d. Alden v. Maine

19. The Violence against Women law was ruled
     a. constitutional in Kimel v. Florida.
     b. constitutional in Alden v. Maine.
     c. unconstitutional in U.S. v. Morrison.
     d. unconstitutional in Printz v. U.S.

20. The diversity of our federal system means that citizens
    a. will get unfair prison sentences.
    b. will get unequal welfare payments.
    c. will get unequal educations funding.
    d. will be able to "vote with their feet" to obtain policies they prefer.

Short Essay Questions. Briefly address the major concepts raised by the following questions.

1. Discuss the three ways of organizing relations between a central government and local governmental units.

2. Identify and explain the division of powers between the national and state governments in the Constitution.

3. Trace and explain the debate over the division of powers between national and state government since the Civil War.

4. Discuss the latest trends in our federal system, including federal mandates and Supreme Court decisions.

ANSWERS TO THE PRACTICE EXAM

Fill-in-the-Blank.

1. federal
2. inherent
3. reserved
4. prohibited powers
5. preempt
6. implied
7. block
8. dual federalism
9. welfare
10. federal mandates

True/False.

1. T	3. F	5. F	7. F	9. T
2. F	4. T	6. T	8. F	10. T

Multiple Choice.

1. c	6. a	11. b	16. a
2. c	7. a	12. b	17. b
3. b	8. d	13. a	18. d
4. b	9. d	14. c	19. c
5. b	10. a	15. a	20. d

Short Essay.

An adequate short answer consists of several paragraphs that relate to concepts addressed by the question. Always demonstrate your knowledge of the ideas by giving examples. The following represent major ideas that should be included in the short essay answer.

1. Discuss the three ways of organizing relations between a central government and local governmental units.

    - Refer to Figure 3-1 for a view of the three ways and how power flows in each.
    - Unitary system in which a centralized government gives some powers to local or sub-divisional governments.
    - Confederal system in which a league of independent states gives some power to the central Federal system in which power is divided between a central government.
    - Federal system in which power is divided between a central government and regional or sub-divisional governments.

2. Identify and explain the division of powers between the national and state governments in the Constitution.

    - Expressed or enumerated powers are national government powers from Article 1, Section 8.
    - Implied powers are national government powers from the necessary and proper clause.
    - Concurrent powers are powers shared by national and state government.
    - Reserved powers are state powers from the 10th amendment to the Constitution.
    - Supremacy clause makes federal law supreme over conflicting state and local law.

3. Trace and explain the debate over the division of powers between national and state government since the Civil War.

    - Dual federalism is the system of government in which the states and national government each remain supreme within their own spheres.
    - Cooperative federalism is the system in which the states and national government should cooperate in solving problems. Federal grants-in-aid are the main factor in developing cooperative federalism.
    - Picket-fence Federalism involves national, state, and local government.

4. Discuss the latest trends in our federal system, including federal mandates and Supreme Court decisions.

    - Federal mandates are a requirement that forces states and local government to comply with certain rules and are a major barrier to new federalism.
    - Printz v. U.S. case struck down the provision of the Brady bill that required state employees to check the background of prospective handgun purchasers.
    - U.S. v. Lopez case held that the Gun-Free School Zones Act in 1990 exceeded Congress's authority under the commerce clause of the constitution.
    - The Supreme Court rules that Congress has overstepped its authority under the commerce clause and 10th and 11th Amendments in the case of United States v. Morrison, Alden v. Maine, and Kimel v. Florida Board of Regents.

Chapter 4
CIVIL LIBERTIES

CHAPTER SUMMARY

Civil Liberties and the Fear of Government

Civil liberties refer to restraining the government's actions against individual rights outlined in the Bill of Rights. A few rights, like prohibiting ex post facto laws are found in Article I, Section 9 of the Constitution.

Extending The Bill of Rights To State Governments

Most citizens are not aware that the Bills of Rights originally applied only to the national government. The 14th Amendment ratified in 1868 seemed to apply civil liberties guaranteed by the national constitution to the states. Incorporation theory holds that the protections of the Bill of Rights are applied to state governments by the 14th Amendment's due process clause. The Supreme Court has gradually and not completely accepted this theory. The first right to be incorporated was freedom of speech in Gitlow v. New York (1925).

Freedom of Religion

The First Amendment to the Constitution begins with two basic principles of freedom of religion. The first is the no establishment clause and the second is the free exercise of religion. The First Amendment begins with the words, "Congress shall make no law respecting an establishment of religion." The establishment clause or a "wall of separation of church and state," as Thomas Jefferson called it, covers such conflicts as state and local aid to religion, school prayer, and teaching of evolution versus creationism. In Lemon v. Kurtzman (1971), the Supreme Court ruled that direct state aid could not be used to subsidize religious instruction. This case created a three-part test for the no establishment clause. In Agostini v. Felton (1997), the Court reversed itself and ruled that federal funds for disadvantaged students attending religious schools did not violate the no establishment clause. The use of public fund school vouchers for religious education has so far been upheld by the Supreme Court, but important issues remain. In the Engel v. Vitale case (1962), the court ruled that school sponsored prayer was a violation of the no establishment clause. Wallace v. Jaffree (1985) struck down a minute of silent prayer in Alabama. Prayer outside the classroom was also limited in Lee v. Weisman (1992) in graduation ceremonies and Santa Fe I.S.D. v. Doe for pre-football game prayers. The issue of teaching creationism was decided in the Edwards v. Aguillard case (1987), which ruled teaching the biblical story of creation was a violation of the no establishment clause. In recent years, the Supreme Court seemed to be lowering the barrier between church and state. In 1995, in Rosenberger v. University of Virginia, the Court ruled that the University must fund a Christian newsletter if funding other campus groups' newsletters.

The free exercise clause has usually focused on striking a balance between religious belief and religious practice. Religious practices can be regulated, as the case of Oregon v. Smith (1990), two Native-American drug counselors were fired for using peyote, an illegal drug, in their religious services. In 1997, the Boerne. v. Flores case ruled the Religious Freedom Restoration Act (RFRA) as unconstitutional for granting religious authorities too much power.

Freedom of Expression

Freedom of expression is probably the most used right that Americans have, but this right cannot be used to say anything at any time and any place. The Supreme Court has established some reasonable restrictions on free speech. The clear and present danger test from the **Schenck v. U.S.** case (1919) restricted speech that provokes a "clear and present danger" to public order. The bad-tendency rule from **Gitlow v. N.Y.** (1925) set a limit on speech that might lead to some evil. Prior restraint to regulate speech, which is censorship, has usually been ruled unconstitutional by the Court. Prior restraint also involves newspapers, movies, and TV shows. In one of the most famous cases, **New York Times v. U.S.** (1971), the Pentagon Papers case, the Supreme Court ruled the New York Times had the right to publish the information about the Vietnam War. The Court has also given protection to symbolic and commercial speech, which involve the use of symbols to express opposition to the government and free speech protection for advertising statements. In a highly controversial case, **Texas v. Johnson** (1989), flag burning was given protection as symbolic speech. Clear areas of speech have not been considered constitutionally protected. These areas include obscenity, slander, fighting words, and hecklers' veto. The Supreme Court in **Miller v. California** (1973) created a four-part list of requirements for determining obscenity. In 2002, the Supreme Court in **Ashcroft v. Free Speech Coalition** ruled the Child Pornography Prevention Act of 1996 was unconstitutional. Slander and libel are wrongfully injuring a person's reputation. Slander is spoken, and libel is written. Look for Court cases under freedom of the press. Fighting words and hecklers' veto are examples of individuals using their freedom of speech to deny rights to others. The Court has almost always ruled this type of speech unconstitutional.

Freedom of the Press
Freedom of the press can be viewed as printed speech, which means many concepts of freedom of expression apply to the press. Libel is the written defamation of a person's character. This is a major concern of mass media today. The Supreme Court in **New York Times v. Sullivan** (1964) gave some protection to media by ruling that public figures who sue for libel must prove actual malice on the part of the media. This greater burden of proof for public figures allows for the criticism of public officials and discussions of differences of opinion without fear of lawsuits. Another important issue for free press is the conflict between the public's right to know and the rights of individuals or the police in the criminal justice system. In **Gannett Company v. De Pasquale** (1979), the Supreme Court ruled that a judge could issue a gag order to protect a defendant's right to a fair trial, from excessive news publicity. The broadcast media, radio, TV, and movies, generally have more restrictions than print media because of the creation of the Federal Communication Commission regulations. The equal time rule, personal attack rule, and fairness doctrine provide for broadcast media to all and try to present both sides of an issue.

The Right to Assemble and to Petition the Government
This right often involves speech and press issues, since few demonstrations involve silent protests. The key issue is, how to balance this right, with the necessity for public officials to control traffic and maintain public order. The Supreme Court, in **Smith v. Collin** (1978), upheld the right of Nazis to march in the Chicago area, when they had been denied a parade permit by the city of Skokie, Illinois. [p. 126-127]

More Liberties under Scrutiny: Privacy Rights
The right to privacy has no explicit mention in the Constitution. It stems from the Supreme Court case, **Griswold v. Connecticut** (1965). The Court ruled that right to privacy stems from "penumbras" in the First, Third, Fourth, Fifth, and Ninth Amendments in the Bill of Rights. The information age, and the vast amount of information on the average citizen, has brought concern with privacy rights to the forefront of the public agenda. The first major application of privacy rights was **Roe v. Wade** (1973), in which the Supreme Court accepted the argument that laws against abortion violate a woman's right to privacy. This decision has created probably the most divisive public policy issue in America, even though later Court decisions placed restrictions on abortion rights. A second major application of right to privacy is the right to die. The New Jersey Supreme Court in the **Quinlan** case in 1976 established this principle. The U.S. Supreme Court modified this concept in **Cruzan v. Director, Missouri Department of Health** (1990). The Cruzan case has led to the creation of "living wills" and other documents to provide safeguards to the right to die. In a related issue, the Court has left the right to assisted suicide to state government, which only Oregon allows. The September 11 attacks have produced an emphasis on security issues, which has led to "roving" wiretaps.

The Great Balancing Act: The Rights of the Accused versus the Rights of Society
One of the most difficult areas of the constitution to balance the rights of individuals and the rights of society is in the rights of those accused of criminal offenses. The Fourth, Fifth, Sixth and Eight Amendments deal with the rights of criminal defendants. [See a complete listing of these rights on p. 137-8.] During the 1960's, the Supreme Court greatly expanded the rights of accused persons. In 1963, Gideon v. Wainwright granted a poor defendant the right to an attorney in most cases. In 1966, Miranda v. Arizona required police to inform an individual of their constitutional rights prior to questioning. Recent Court decisions have placed some restrictions on the Miranda ruling in a continuing effort to find the right balance between individual and societal rights. The exclusionary rule, which prohibited the admission of illegally obtained evidence during a trial, was applied to federal court in 1914. The concept was first applied to state courts in the case of Mapp v. Ohio (1961). Refer back to Table 4-1 for incorporation cases. Recent Court decisions have provided some discretion for police officers who are acting in "good faith." The Death Penalty is one of the most debated aspects of our criminal justice system because of the 8th Amendment protection against "cruel and unusual" punishment. In

1972, the Supreme Court ruled in Furman v. Georgia that the death penalty was random and arbitrary. This case was based on the existing state laws of the death penalty, which have been changed and today exist in 38 states. [See Figure 4-1.] In 1996, Congress passed the Anti-Terrorism and Effective death Penalty Act. This sharply reduced the time for death-row appeals. The growth of the Internet will produce new challenges in defining free expression rights. Hate speech is very difficult to deal with. The exercise of religious rights, particularly in institutions like schools, continues to stir controversy. The protection of privacy rights in our online culture and the issues of abortion and the right to die continue to defy solutions. Crime will continue to be a problem as our society looks for new ways to balance the rights of the accused with the rights of us all.

The Death Penalty

This section discusses the death penalty—is it cruel and unusual punishment? Time limits for death row inmates.

Civil Liberties: Why Are They Important Today?

In the past, every time there was a crisis, civil liberties were jeopardized. Today, we are in a time of crisis because of the war on terrorism and civil liberties are threatened. We must not take our civil liberties for granted. After September 11, over 1,100 foreign nationals were detained in the United States.

KEY TERMS

Actual malice — p. 130
Arraignment — p. 137
Civil Liberties — p. 113
Clear and present danger — p. 125
Commercial speech — p. 124
Defamation of character p.128
Establishment clause — p. 115
Exclusionary rule — p. 140

Free exercise clause — p. 121
Gag order — p. 131
Incorporation theory — p. 114
Libel — p. 130
Prior restraint — p. 122
Public figures — p. 130
Slander — p. 128
Symbolic speech — p. 124
Writ of *habeas corpus* — p. 137

PRACTICE EXAM
(Answers appear at the end of this chapter.)

Fill-in-the-Blank.   Supply the missing word(s) or term to complete the sentence.

1.   _____ _____ involve restraining the government's actions against individuals.

2.   It was not until the _____ Amendment was ratified that our Constitution explicitly guaranteed due process of law to everyone.

3.   The Lemon Test explains the concept of the _____ _____ in freedom of religion.

4.   According to the _____ _____ rule, speech or other First Amendment freedoms may be curtailed if there is a possibility that such expression might lead to some evil.

5.   The burning of the American flag as part of a peaceful protest is expressive conduct considered _____ _____.

6.   For slander to be judged as defamation of character there must be a _____ _____ witness.

7.   Only when a statement is made with_____ _____ can a public official receive damages for libel.

8.   A newer controversy surrounding illegal searches involves _____ wiretaps.

9. The _____, _____, _____, and _____ Amendments specially deal with the rights of criminal defendants.

10. The use of illegally seized evidence is prohibited in a trial because of the _____ rule.

True/False. Circle the appropriate letter to indicate if the statement is true or false.

T (F) 1. The concept of civil liberties mainly refers to laws passed by Congress to limit government power.

(T) F 2. As originally presented, the Bill of Rights limited only the powers of the states, not the national government.

(T) F 3. Most of the guarantees in the Bill of Rights now apply to the fifty states.

T (F) 4. The Supreme Court has generally accepted the use of state aid to private religious schools.

T (F) 5. For the most part, Americans are very limited in their ability to criticize public officials.

(T) F 6. The federal courts have not extended constitutional protections of free speech that is considered obscene.

(T) F 7. Gag orders restrict the publication of news about a trial in progress or a pretrial hearing.

T (F) 8. The right of privacy is explicitly guaranteed in the Bill of Rights.

T (F) 9. The Webster and Planned Parenthood decisions have made it much easier to obtain a legal abortion.

(T) F 10. The United States has one of the highest violent crime rates in the world.

Multiple Choice. Circle the correct response.

1. When we are speaking of civil liberties, we are referring to limitations on government as outlined in the
   a. Declaration of Independence.
   b. Magna Carta.
   c. Articles of Confederation.
   d. Bill of Rights.

2. The view that most of the protections of the Bill of Rights are included under the fourteenth Amendment's protection against state government is called the
   a. inclusionary theory.
   b. nullification theory.
   c. necessary and proper theory.
   d. incorporation theory.

3. The three-part Lemon test concerns the issue of
   a. symbolic speech.
   b. state aid to church-related schools.
   c. presentation of evidence before a grand jury.
   d. the right-to-die.

4. The free exercise clause in the First Amendment does not prevent the government from curtailing religious practices that
    a.   work against public policy and the public welfare.
    b.   infringe on citizen's sensitivities.
    c.   are defined by media as "cult" religions.
    d.   are a willful violation of the Pledge of Allegiance at public school.

5. According to the "clear and present danger" test,
    a.   a speech must be unclear as to its intent for it to be ruled unconstitutional.
    b.   the action called for must be constitutionally "vague" in order to be ruled unconstitutional.
    c.   free speech can be curbed if such speech would cause a condition that Congress has the power to prevent.
    d.   free speech may not be curbed, because speech alone cannot bring about action.

6. The burning of an American flag in a peaceful protest is an example of
    a.   a violation of the Constitution.
    b.   a protected action under the clear and present danger concept.
    c.   a protected action under the symbolic speech concept.
    d.   an issue not yet decided by the Supreme Court.

7. Paid advertising can be constitutionally protected as a form of
    a.   commercial speech.
    b.   symbolic speech.
    c.   exempted speech.
    d.   private speech.

8. The Miller v. California case created a list of requirements that apply to
    a.   abortion.
    b.   religious freedom.
    c.   obscenity.
    d.   libel.

9. In Edwards v. Aguillard, the Supreme Court declared a Louisiana law unconstitutional because the law
    a.   violated the Lemon Test.
    b.   promoted a particular religion.
    c.   violated the 14th amendment.
    d.   promoted secular education.

10. Public officials may sue for libel if they can prove the statement
    a.   was false.
    b.   hurt the official's reputation.
    c.   hurt the official's feelings.
    d.   was made with actual malice.

11. Gag orders are
    a.   designed to eliminate illegal speech.
    b.   designed to eliminate unlawful assembly.
    c.   restrictions on the publication of news concerning pretrial hearing or trials in progress.
    d.   part of the controversy over the death penalty.

12. The Roe v. Wade case decided the abortion issue on the basis of
    a.   freedom of religion.
    b.   freedom of speech.
    c.   right to privacy.
    d.   the incorporation concept.

13. The Exclusionary rule prohibits
    a. defendants from testifying in their own behalf.
    b. improperly obtained evidence from being used by prosecutors.
    c. a spouse from testifying in a criminal case.
    d. the defense counsel form having access to the prosecution's evidence.

14. The Exclusionary rule was first extended to state court proceedings in the Supreme Court case of
    a. Nix v. Williams.
    b. Miranda v. Arizona.
    c. Mapp v. Ohio.
    d. Betts v. Brady.

15. A technically incorrect search warrant can be legal under the concept of
    a. the Miranda rule.
    b. the "good faith" exception.
    c. the unreasonable search and seizure.
    d. the right to an attorney if you cannot afford one.

16. The case that ruled against the right to commit suicide was
    a. Cruzan v. Director, Missouri Dept. of Health.
    b. Furman v. Georgia.
    c. Washington v. Glucksberg.
    d. Miranda v. Arizona.

17. The Anti-Terrorism and Effective Death Penalty Act provided for
    a. immediate execution after the guilty verdict.
    b. execution within a month after the guilty verdict.
    c. a severe time limit on death-row appeals.
    d. the so called "three strikes" and you are out procedure.

18. According to the text, a growing concern about free speech on the Internet is
    a. slander.
    b. obscenity.
    c. hate speech.
    d. fraud in commercial speech.

19. In the case of Doe v. University of Michigan (1989), the Court ruled the campus speech code was
    a. not covered by the U.S. Constitution.
    b. constitutional.
    c. constitutional with equal time for both sides.
    d. unconstitutional.

20. The Supreme Court in 2000 ruled that "partial-birth" abortions are
    a. unconstitutional.
    b. not covered by Roe v. Wade.
    c. constitutional.
    d. constitutional, only if passed by state legislatures.

Short Essay Questions   Briefly address the major concepts raised by the following questions.

1. Explain the historical context for the importance of the Bill of Rights within the Constitution.

2. Identify and explain the two concepts of freedom of religion contained in the First Amendment.

3. Discuss the important principles established by the Supreme Court for freedom of speech and press.

4. Outline and discuss the rights of an individual accused of a crime.

ANSWERS TO THE PRACTICE EXAM

Fill-in-the-blank.

1. Civil Liberties
2. Fourteenth
3. establishment
4. bad-tendency
5. symbolic
6. third party
7. actual malice
8. physician
9. Fourth, Fifth, Sixth, Eighth
10. exclusionary

True/False.

1. F	3. T	5. F	7. T	9. F
2. T	4. F	6. T	8. F	10. T

Multiple Choice.

1. d	6. c	11. c	16. c
2. d	7. a	12. c	17. c
3. b	8. c	13. b	18. c
4. a	9. b	14. c	19. d
5. c	10. d	15. b	20. c

Short Essay.

An adequate short answer consists of several paragraphs that relate to concepts addressed by the question. Always demonstrate your knowledge of the ideas by giving examples. The following represent major ideas that should be included in the short essay answer.

1. Explain the historical context for the importance of the Bill of Rights within the Constitution.

    • Few specific restrictions on government were contained in the constitution.
    • The Bill of Rights did not apply to state governments.
    • The Fourteenth Amendment guaranteed civil liberties of the Constitution applied to the states, which is called incorporation.
    • Only gradually on a case-by-case basis, but never completely, has the Supreme Court accepted incorporation.
    • See Table 4-1 for a list of cases incorporating different constitutional rights

2. Identify and explain the two concepts of freedom of religion contained in the First Amendment.
    • The establishment clause prohibits official government support of religion.
        • Lemon v. Kurtzman (1971) creates a three-part test of this concept. *Lemon*
        • Engle v. Vitale (1962) ruled that official prayer in public school is unconstitutional.
        • Teaching of evolution cannot be banned and bible story of creation cannot be taught.
    • The free exercise of religion shall not be prohibited.

- Religious beliefs are absolute, but religious practices that work against public policy and public welfare may be restricted.
- Oregon v. Smith (1990) ruled that Native Americans could be denied unemployment benefits when fired from a state job for using peyote in their religious services.
- Congress passed the Religious Freedom Restoration Act (RFRA) in 1993 to require all levels of government to "accommodate religious conduct."
- City of Boerne v. Flores (1997) ruled the RFRA law unconstitutional.

3. Discuss the important principles established by the Supreme Court for freedom of speech and press.
   - Freedom of speech has never been considered absolute, so some restrictions are permitted.
     - Schenck v. U.S. (1919) ruled on speech that provokes a "clear and present danger," saying that Congress has a right to prevent this type of speech and it is not constitutionally protected.
     - Gitlow v. New York (1925) held that expression that might lead to some "evil" is not protected.
     - However, in the New York Times v. U.S. (1971), the court ruled that prior restraint or censorship is unconstitutional.
   - Symbolic speech and commercial speech have received constitutional protection.
     - Texas v. Johnson (1989) ruled that the burning of an American flag in a peaceful protest is protected as symbolic speech.
   - Some speech has never been constitutionally protected.
     - Miller v. California (1973) established a formal list of requirements for obscenity, which is not protected.
     - Slander, the public uttering of a false statement that harms a person's reputation, is not protected.
     - Fighting words and heckler's veto are examples of using speech to prevent others from exercising their rights and are not protected.
   - Freedom of the press can be viewed as printed speech, so many of the same concepts apply.
     - Libel is the written defamation of a person's reputation, but the press has some limited protection from libel.
     - The New York Times v. Sullivan (1964) created the concept of a public figure, who must prove actual malice on the part of media, to be able to sue for libel.
     - Another significant free press issue is conflict between free press and a criminal suspect's right to a fair trial. Gannett Company v. De Pasquale (1979), provided for judges to issue gag order to restrict the publication of news about pretrial hearings or trials in progress.
     - Broadcast media has generally not been protected like published materials. The federal Communication Commission (FCC) has created guidelines such as the equal time rule, personal attack rule, and the fairness doctrine.

4. Outline and discuss the right of an individual accused of a crime.
   - In the Bill of Rights, the 4th, 5th, 6th, and 8th Amendments deal with rights of criminal defendants. The process is divided into three parts.
     1. Limits on the conduct of police officers and prosecutors
     2. Defendant's pretrial rights
     3. Trial rights
   - The 4th Amendment protects against an unreasonable search and seizure of evidence.
   - The exclusionary rule prevents this evidence from being admitted at trial. Mapp v. Ohio extended the exclusionary rule to state courts.
   - The 5th Amendment provides for the right to remain silent, to be informed of the charges, and the right to legal counsel. Miranda v. Arizona dealt with the right to be informed of your rights.
   - The 6th Amendment provides for legal counsel during a trial, even if the defendant cannot afford one. Betts v. Brady applied this to capital cases. Gideon v. Wainwright applied this to felony offenses.

Chapter 5
CIVIL RIGHTS

CHAPTER SUMMARY

Civil Rights are the rights of all Americans to equal treatment under law, as provided in the Fourteenth Amendment to the Constitution. Essentially, the history of civil rights in America is the struggle of various groups to be free from discriminatory treatment.

African Americans and the Consequences of Slavery in the United States

Before 1863, the Constitution protected slavery. In *Dred Scott v. Sanford* (1857), the Supreme Court had upheld the constitutionality of slavery by ruling that slaves were not citizens of the United States. President Lincoln's Emancipation Proclamation in 1863 and the passage of the 13th, 14th, and 15th Amendments to the Constitution ended constitutional inequality. From 1865-1875, to protect African-American rights from being violated by state government, the Republican-controlled Congress passed several Civil Rights Acts. The Supreme Court ruled these acts unconstitutional, so they were largely ineffective. The most significant of these decisions was *Plessy v. Ferguson* (1896), which created the doctrine of separate-but-equal and led to racial segregation, particularly in the South. When federal troops that occupied the South were withdrawn in 1877, the Southern states restricted African-Americans' right to vote by imposing a number of laws, such as the grandfather clause, poll taxes, and literacy tests. The white primary law was finally ruled unconstitutional in the 1944 case of *Smith v. Allwright.* The end to the separate-but-equal doctrine and racial segregation began in the 1930s with a series of lawsuits to admit African Americans to graduate and professional schools. These lawsuits culminated in the unanimous Supreme Court decision in *Brown v. Board of Education of Topeka* in 1954, which ruled that public school segregation of the races violates the equal protection clause of the 14th Amendment. In reaction to this decision, state governments sought loopholes in the decision, and society witnessed a tremendous increase in private, often religion-based schools. The early attempts to integrate schools often relied on court-ordered busing of students across neighborhoods. Recently, the federal courts have returned authority to local school officials, as in *Missouri v. Jenkins* (1995), which allowed Missouri to stop financing a magnet school for racial integration.

The Civil Rights Movement

The *Brown* decision was a moral victory but did little to change the underlying structure of segregation. In 1955, an African-American woman named Rosa Parks refused to give up her seat on the bus to a white man. She was arrested and fined. Thus began the civil rights protests that would eventually end racial segregation. Martin Luther King, Jr., a Baptist minister, organized a yearlong boycott of the Montgomery, Alabama bus line, the success of which propelled King to national leadership of the civil rights movement. The culmination of the movement came in 1963, when intending to influence Civil rights legislation then pending in Congress, Dr. King led a march on Washington D.C. and gave his famous "I have a dream" speech.

Modern Civil Rights Legislation

In passing the Civil Rights Act of 1964, Congress had created the most far-reaching bill on civil rights in modern times. The Act demolished discrimination in all areas, except housing, which was covered in the Civil Rights Act of 1968. [See p. 160 for the major provisions of the Act.] Congress followed up the 1964 Act with the Voting Rights Act of 1965, which eliminated discriminatory voter-registration laws and authorized federal officials to register voters, primarily in the South. Subsequent amendments to the Voting Rights Act granted protections, such as bilingual ballots, to other minorities. Although there is increased voting participation among all minorities, there are lingering social and economic disparities.

Women's Struggle for Equal Rights

Women first became involved politically in the abolition of slavery movement. From this effort, Lucretia Mott and Elizabeth Cady Stanton organized the first women's rights convention in 1848. The 1870 campaign to ratify the 15th Amendment, which gave voting rights to African-American men, split the women's suffrage movement. But women successfully campaigned for passage of the 19th Amendment, which enfranchised women and was ratified in 1920. After achieving the right to vote, women engaged in little political activity until the 1960s, when the feminist movement called for political, economic, and social equality for women. The feminist movement attempted to obtain the ratification of an Equal Rights Amendment in the 1970s, but the necessary 38 states failed to ratify. After this defeat, the women's movement began to work for women's increased representation in government. Political Action Committees, PACs, were created to fund women candidates. The largest of these PACs is EMILY's list, which stands for "Early Money Is Like Yeast—It Makes the Dough Rise." Although no major political party has nominated a woman for president, women have run for the vice-presidency and serve as members of the cabinet and the Supreme Court. Women have been elected governors of major states, mayors of large cities, and about 22% are state legislators. In 2002, a woman was elected to a leadership post in Congress. Nancy Pelosi (D) California was elected Democrats minority whip in the U.S. House of Representatives.

Gender-Based Discrimination in the Workplace
Title VII of the Civil Rights Act of 1964 prohibited gender discrimination in employment, including sexual harassment. In 1991, it became apparent that these laws were not being vigorously enforced when Anita Hill charged Supreme Court nominee Clarence Thomas with sexual harassment. This publicity resulted in an increasing number of court cases dealing with sexual harassment. Supreme Court cases like *Faragher v. City of Boca Raton* (1998), and *Burlington Industries v. Ellerth* (1998), ruled that employers and employees were libel for sexual harassment if they did not exercise reasonable care to prevent and correct promptly any sexually harassing behavior. Another important issue for women in the workplace has been wage discrimination. Although the Equal Pay Act of 1963 was designed to provide for equal pay, a woman earns about seventy-eight cents for every dollar earned by a man. Some of the key reasons for this are the low pay for jobs traditionally held by women (such as childcare) and the corporate "glass ceiling" that prevents women from reaching the highest executive positions in business.

Civil Rights: Beyond Equal Protection
Minority groups and women granted equality by the Civil Rights Act of 1964 sometimes lacked the education and skills, because of past discrimination, to compete for educational admissions and jobs.

Affirmative Action
The government responding to remedy this situation created Affirmative Action in 1965. Affirmative Action is a policy to give special consideration to traditionally disadvantaged groups in an effort to overcome present effect of past discrimination. This policy ran into serious problems in 1978 in the Supreme Court case of **Regents of the University of California v. Bakke**, which involved admission policies at UC-Davis Medical School. Alan Bakke argued that the affirmative action admission policy requiring a racial quota was reverse discrimination against those who do not have minority status. The Supreme Court agreed. A number of cases in the 1980s and 1990s put even further limitations on affirmative action. In the 1995 Adarand Constructors Inc. v. Pena case, the Court ruled that any affirmative action program that uses racial or ethnic classifications for making decisions would be under "strict scrutiny." In the **Hopwood v. State of Texas** case (1996), the Supreme Court ruled that any use of race to give an admission to law school was unconstitutional. Also in 1996, Proposition 209 was passed by the voters of California, ending all state-sponsored affirmative action programs. Majority public opinion still seems to favor affirmative action programs because it is apparent that the effects of discrimination continue today and perhaps not all discrimination is in the past.

Special Protection for Older Americans
Age discrimination is potentially the most widespread form of discrimination because it can affect everyone at some point in life. Congress passed the Age Discrimination Employment Act in 1967. This law protects workers over the age of 40, and an amendment to the law passed in 1978 prohibited mandatory retirement of most workers under the age of 70. In early 2000, in the **Kimel v. Florida Board of Regents** case limits the ADEA, making it no longer applicable to state employees. Older Americans have fought discrimination by registering and voting as the first rank among any age group. The largest interest group in America is **AARP**, which protects the rights of individuals 50 years of age and older.

Securing Rights for Persons with Disabilities
Older Americans and persons with disabilities did not have rights protected by the Civil Rights Act of 1964. The landmark legislation to protect rights of persons with disabilities was the Americans with Disabilities Act of 1990 (ADA). This law requires employers to "reasonably accommodate" the needs of persons with

disabilities. This has required physical access, which has led to increased facilities costs for government and business. These costs and the difficulty of interpreting the ADA have caused controversy. In 1998, the Supreme Court ruled that persons infected with HIV, the virus that causes AIDS, are under the protection of the ADA.

The Rights and Status of Gay Males and Lesbians

The "Stonewall Riot" in 1969, in which gays and lesbians fought with police after a raid at a gay bar, created the movement for gay and lesbian rights. The movement has changed state laws on sexual relations between consenting adults, and in ten states and over 165 cities and counties that have special laws against gay and lesbian discrimination. In a 1996 Supreme Court decision in **Romer v. Evans**, the Court overturned a law that would not protect homosexuals from discrimination. The growth of the political activity of gays has not escaped the notice of politicians. Conservatives have generally been against gay rights, while liberals like Jesse Jackson have supported gay rights. President Clinton in 1997 became the first sitting president to address a gay rights organization. President Clinton was a leading force in developing a "Don't Ask, Don't Tell" policy to allow gays and lesbians to have careers in the military. Probably the most controversial aspect of gay rights is same-sex marriages and child custody issues. The Hawaii Supreme Court seems to have cleared the way for same-sex marriages in Hawaii. Other states have passed laws banning these marriages. In 1996, Congress passed the Defense of Marriage Act, which bans federal recognition of same-sex marriages.

The Rights and Status of Juveniles

Children, defined as persons under the age sixteen, and in some cases under 18 or 21, have generally not had the same legal protection as adults. The reason for this lack of protections is the assumption by society that their parents basically protect children. The Supreme Court began a slow evolution of children's rights with the **Brown v. Board of Education of Topeka** case, which was fully discussed in Chapter 5. The Brown case granted children the status of rights-bearing persons. In **Yoder v. Wisconsin** in 1972, the Court ruled, "children are 'persons' within the meaning of the Bill of Rights." The Twenty-sixth Amendment to the U.S. Constitution, which was ratified in 1971, granted the right to vote to citizens who are eighteen years old. The fact that eighteen year olds could be drafted and sent to fight and possibly die in Vietnam seemed to be a key factor in lowering the voting age. In civil and criminal cases, the age of majority, which is the right to manage one's own affairs and have full enjoyment of civil rights, will vary from eighteen to twenty-one years, depending on the state. In criminal cases, the concept of common law is that children from 7 to 14 years cannot commit a crime because they are not mature enough to understand what they are doing. Recent heinous crimes, such as the shooting deaths of four students and a teacher at a school in Jonesboro, Arkansas, by an 11 year old and a 13 year old, have caused some state officials to consider lowering the age at which a juvenile may be tried as an adult and faced with adult penalties, including the death penalty.

Civil Rights: Why Are They Important Today?

While African Americans, minorities, and women have made major gains since 1950, they remain under-represented in national politics and participation. The debate over the melting pot of cultures versus ethnic separatism or multiculturalism will continue. The role of women in the workplace and equal pay issues will continue to be a focus of national domestic policy The expanding proportion of the population that is over the age of sixty-five will continue to struggle against age discrimination. Persons with disabilities will continue to find new areas of employment and physical access that will challenge the definitions of the Americans with disabilities Act. Clearly, discrimination continues against gay and lesbian persons and needs to be addressed. The debate of the rights of children will continue as the nation struggles with the problems of child abuse and violent crimes committed on others by children.

KEY TERMS

Affirmative action — p.170
busing — p. 156
civil law — p. 179
civil disobedience — p. 158
civil rights — p. 151
common law — p. 180
criminal law — p. 179

de facto segregation — p. 156
de jure segregation — p. 156
feminism — p. 164
gender discrimination — p. 166
Grandfather Clause — p. 154
literacy test — p. 154

majority — p. 179
mandatory retirement — p.172
necessaries — p.179
poll tax — p. 154
reverse discrimination — p. 170
separate-but-equal — p. 153

sexual harassment — p. 168
subpoena — p. 160
suffrage — p. 164
white primary — p. 154

PRACTICE EXAM
(Answers appear at the end of this chapter.)

Fill-in-the-Blank. Supply the missing word(s) or term(s) to complete the sentence.

1. In _____ v. _____, the Supreme Court confirmed the constitutionality of slavery.

2. The constitutional principle that permitted racial segregation was called the _____ _____ _____ _____.

3. The obvious solution to both de facto and de jure segregation of schools was _____.

4. Martin Luther King Jr.'s philosophy of _____ included such tactics as demonstrations and marches.

5. The _____ _____ _____ of 1964 was the most far-reaching civil rights bill in modern times.

6. The _____ _____ _____ of 1965 outlawed discriminatory voter-registration tests.

7. The Civil Rights Act of 1964 prohibits discrimination against any person because of race, color, or _____ _____.

8. The first political cause in which women became actively engaged was the movement to _____ _____.

9. The Civil Rights Act of 1968 forbade discrimination in most _____.

10. Barriers faced by women in the corporate world are referred to as the _____ _____.

True/False. Circle the appropriate letter to indicate if the statement is true or false.

T   F   1. The case of *Plessy v. Ferguson* created the separate-but-equal doctrine.

T   F   2. The Reconstruction statutes after the Civil War helped to secure civil rights for African-Americans equal to those of whites.

T   F   3. Concentrations of minorities in defined geographic locations results in *de facto* segregation.

T   F   4. The era of civil rights protests in the mid 1950s began with the boycott of public bus transportation in Montgomery, Alabama.

T   F   5. The white primary was used in southern states to deny African-Americans the right to vote.

T   F   6. African-Americans increased their political participation as a direct result of the Civil Rights Act of 1964.

T   F   7. A Gallup Poll taken in 2004 showed that 95 percent of the public would vote for an African-American for president.

T   F   8. During the national debate over the ratification of the ERA, a women's countermovement to feminism emerged.

T   F   9.   No woman has ever held a leadership position in Congress.

T   F   10. Gender discrimination was prohibited by the Civil Rights Act of 1964.

Multiple-Choice. Circle the correct response.

1. The *Dred Scott* case
   a. freed the slaves in the South.
   b. contributed to a more peaceful resolution of the slavery issue.
   c. contributed to making the Civil War inevitable.
   d. provided full and equal citizenship for all African Americans.

2. The reconstruction statutes had the effect of
   a. securing equality for African Americans in their civil rights.
   b. doing little to secure equality for African Americans in their civil rights.
   c. restructuring society to provide for greater equality of opportunity.
   d. setting the stage for the Civil War.

3. The effect of *Plessy v. Ferguson* on racial segregation was to establish a
   a. "clear and present danger" principle to further integration.
   b. pattern to outlaw segregation in the South.
   c. pattern for racial integration throughout the country.
   d. constitutional cornerstone of racial discrimination throughout the country.

4. An unintended effect of the Supreme Court's direction of "all deliberate speed" toward achieving integration in public education was that it
   a. allowed some jurisdictions to integrate too quickly thereby causing confusion.
   b. provided the pattern for complete integration of public education.
   c. was used as a loophole by some jurisdictions to stall efforts toward integration.
   d. created an influx of rural students attending urban schools.

5. *De facto* segregation of school districts can come about through
   a. residential concentration of minorities in defined geographical locations.
   b. school boards drawing boundary lines to include only certain minority groups.
   c. Supreme Court edicts.
   d. a program of forced busing across district lines.

6. Recent Supreme Court decisions on busing to integrate public schools have emphasized
   a. more busing to integrate schools fully.
   b. spending more money to attract minority students without busing.
   c. stronger court controls over local schools.
   d. restoring more control to local schools.

7. Discrimination in most housing was forbidden by the
   a. Civil Rights Act of 1964.
   b. Civil Rights Act of 1968.
   c. Voting Rights Act of 1965.
   d. Equal Housing Act of 1965.

8. The first African American candidate to compete seriously for the presidential nomination was
   a. Jesse Jackson.
   b. Clarence Thomas.
   c. Thurgood Marshall.
   d. Colin Powell.

9. In terms of the women's movement in the U.S., the anti-slavery movement had the effect of
    a. retarding organized political action by women.
    b. enslaving women and creating a secondary status for them.
    c. creating the first political cause in which women could become actively engaged.
    d. allowing women to become the dominant force in this movement.

10. In which country did women first earn the right to vote first?
    a. New Zealand
    b. The United States
    c. Canada
    d. Mexico

11. President Clinton appointed _____ women to his cabinet.
    a. no
    b. six
    c. four
    d. three

12. The Equal Rights Amendment was first introduced in Congress in
    a. 1966.
    b. 1772.
    c. 1944.
    d. 1923.

13. Sexual harassment of women in the workplace is
    a. no longer prohibited by statute.
    b. prohibited by Title VII of the Civil Rights Act of 1964.
    c. considered "protective" legislation that the Supreme Court has ruled unconstitutional.
    d. considered a form of reverse discrimination against men.

14. The Equal Pay Act of 1963 has
    a. never been enforced.
    b. only applied when women and men do exactly the same job.
    c. only applied to comparable worth situations.
    d. totally equalized pay between women and men.

15. The issue of wage discrimination was first addressed
    a. during the Civil War.
    b. during World War I.
    c. during World War II.
    d. during the 1960s.

16. The "glass ceiling" refers to
    a. subtle barriers that prevent women from being promoted to top positions in corporations.
    b. corporate espionage.
    c. reverse discrimination against men.
    d. national laws designed to protect women from wage discrimination.

17. Which President appointed the most women to his cabinet?
    a. George W. Bush
    b. Bill Clinton
    c. Richard Nixon
    d. George H. Bush

18. Which Supreme Court case ruled that Title VII protection applied to harassment by members of the same sex?
    a. Oncale v. Sundowner Offshore Services, Inc.
    b. Harris v. Forklift Systems, Inc.
    c. Faragher v. City of Boca Raton
    d. Burlington Industries v. Ellerth

19. Forced retirement when a person reaches a certain age is called
    a. forced retirement.
    b. age discrimination.
    c. job renewal for youth.
    d. mandatory retirement .

20. Which of the following is a reason for a new civil rights agenda in the U.S.?
    a. People have too many rights today.
    b. Discrimination has just about ended.
    c. The old concepts of majority versus minority are no longer applicable.
    d. War on Terrorism must create inequality.

Short Essay Questions. Briefly address the major concepts raised by the following questions.

1. Explain the impact on education of the Supreme Court's decision in *Brown v. Board of Education of Topeka*, and discuss what new problems the decision fostered.

2. Discuss the key events in the Civil Rights Movement that led to passage of the 1964 Civil Rights Act.

3. Discuss the provisions of the Voting Rights Act of 1965. What impact has this had on political participation among minority voters in the United States?

4. Explain the major issues of gender discrimination in the workplace.

ANSWERS TO THE PRACTICE EXAM

Fill-in-the-Blank.

1. Dred Scott v. Sanford
2. separate-but-equal doctrine
3. busing
4. nonviolence
5. Civil Rights Act
6. Voting Rights Act
7. national origin
8. abolish slavery
9. housing
10. glass ceiling

True/False.

1. T	3. T	5. T	7. T	9. F
2. F	4. T	6. F	8. T	10. T

Multiple Choice.

1.	c	5.	a	9.	c	13.	b	17. b
2.	b	6.	d	10.	a	14.	b	18. a
3.	d	7.	b	11.	c	15.	c	19. d
4.	c	8.	a	12.	d	16.	a	20. c

Short Essay.

An adequate short answer consists of several paragraphs that relate to concepts raised by the question. Always demonstrate your knowledge of the ideas by giving examples. The following represent major ideas that should be included in these short essays.

1. Explain the impact on education of the Supreme Court's decision in *Brown v. Board of Education of Topeka* and discuss what new problems the decision fostered.
   - The concept of separate-but-equal from *Plessy v. Ferguson* was overturned.
   - The order to implement "with all deliberate speed" was used as a loophole by state officials to slow the pace of integration of schools.
   - School integration in Little Rock, Arkansas, was blocked by use of the state's National Guard.
   - President Eisenhower federalized the Arkansas National guard and integrated schools in Little Rock.
   - *De Jure* segregation is illegal under the Brown decision.
   - *De Facto* segregation because of housing patterns is dealt with by busing to achieve integration.

2. Discuss the key events in the Civil Rights Movement that led to the passage of the 1964 Civil Rights Act.
   - Rosa Parks refuses to move to the back of the bus, the "colored" section in Montgomery, Alabama.
   - Martin Luther King, Jr. leads a yearlong African-American boycott of the Montgomery bus line.
   - The Southern Christian Leadership Conference is formed.
   - A series of nonviolent sit-ins, protests, demonstrations, and marches are held.
   - Dr. King is arrested in Birmingham, Alabama, during a protest in which police use dogs and cattle prods on the demonstrators.
   - Media coverage of these events has a profound effect on public opinion.
   - Dr. King organizes a march on Washington, D.C., and delivers his famous "I have a Dream" speech, which is televised to millions.

3. Discuss the provisions of the Voting Rights Act of 1965. How did this law influence the political participation of minority voters in the United States.
   - Provision One outlawed the discriminatory voter-registration test.
   - Provision Two authorized federal registration of voters and federally administered voting procedures.
   - African-American registration and voting increased dramatically.
   - More African Americans became prominent in national politics.
   - Hispanic registration and voting increased dramatically.
   - Bilingual ballots were authorized.

4   Explain the major issues of gender discrimination in the workplace.
   - Title VII of the Civil Rights Act of 1964 prohibits gender discrimination in the workplace.
   - One major issue is sexual harassment. Sexual harassment has been extended to the employer who does nothing to stop sexual harassment by an employee through court decisions in *Faragher v. City of Boca Raton* (1998), and *Burlington Industries v. Ellerth* (1998).
   - Second major issue is wage discrimination. The Equal Pay Act of 1963 prohibits unequal pay for men and women doing the same job. Comparable worth is the concept that takes into account skill, effort, and responsibility to determine pay because traditional "women's" jobs pay less than traditional "men's" jobs. Women have a harder time getting high corporate positions because of the "glass ceiling."

Chapter 6
PUBLIC OPINION AND POLITICAL SOCIALIZATION

CHAPTER SUMMARY
Public opinion clearly plays an important role in our political system. President George W. Bush has had widespread support for his war on terrorism. Two other presidents have shown just how powerful public opinion can be. Opposition to the War in Vietnam seemed to be a factor in 1968, when President Lyndon Johnson declined to run for re-election. Public opinion on the scandal surrounding the 1972 Watergate break-in gave Congress strong support to initiate impeachment proceeding against President Nixon.

Defining Public Opinion
Public opinion is defined as the aggregate of individual attitudes or beliefs shared by some portion of adults. Public opinion is made known in a democracy by protests, demonstrations, and lobbying by interest groups. There are very few issues on which most Americans agree. When a large proportion of the public does appear to hold the same view on an issue, a consensus exists. If opinion is polarized between two quite different positions, divisive opinion exists. Sometimes a poll will show that a large number of people have no opinion because participants either have no information about the subject or are not interested enough in the issue to form a position.

How Public Opinion is Formed: Political Socialization
The process by which individuals acquire political beliefs and opinions is called political socialization. The most important influence in this process is the family. Children have a strong need for parental approval and are very receptive to the parents' opinions. The clearest family influence is the political party identification. Schools are also an important influence. Education seems to influence the level of activity in the political process. The more education a person receives the higher the level of political activity. Friendships and associations in peer groups can influence political attitudes. Religious associations also create political attitudes, although this is hard to measure. In recent years, over 42% of evangelical Protestants are Republicans. Wealth and social status influence political attitudes, although there is probably a strong correlation with the education factor in shaping wealth and social status. When events produce a long-term political impact, you have generational effects, which can influence political opinions. For example, voters who grew up in the 1930s during the Great Depression were likely to become Democrats. Some individuals have the ability to influence the opinions of others because of position, expertise, or personality. Often these individuals, called opinion leaders, use the media to influence opinions. Finally, the election of Ronald Reagan in 1980 seemed to produce a gender gap, in which women were 5 or 6% more likely to vote for Democrats for President. This gap continues into the 2000s.

Political Preferences and Voting Behavior
This section discusses vote choice as related to the voter's political views and preferences. Includes a discussion of demographic influences such as the role of education, economic status, religious influences, race and ethnicity, and gender on one's political preferences and voting behavior. Also discusses the role of party identification and the perception of the candidate in determining vote choice.

Measuring Public Opinion
One of the most common means of gathering and measuring public opinion is through the use of opinion polls. In the 1800s, newspapers and magazines used face-to-face straw polls to attract readers. In the 20th century, the magazine *Literary Digest* developed modern techniques by mailing questionnaires to subscribers. In 1936, the magazine's poll predicted that Alfred Landon would defeat Franklin Roosevelt for President. Landon won only two states. The most important principle in poll taking is randomness. If drawn from a truly random sample of opinions, a poll should be relatively accurate. Gallup and Roper polls interview about 1,500 individuals to get within a margin of error. Public opinion polls are snapshots of opinions at a specific time on a specific question. The timing of the poll, a sampling error of interviewing too few people, and the wording of the question can all create an inaccurate prediction of a political outcome.

Technology and Opinion Polls

During the 1970's, telephone polling began to dominate over in-person polling. The success of the telemarketing industry has caused a huge no response rate on the telephone. The Internet has replaced the telephone as the latest polling technology. It remains to be seen if it goes the way of the telephone.

Public Opinion and the Political Process

Although Americans are divided into numerous ethnic, religious, and political groups, the American political culture binds us together with the core values of (1) liberty, equality, and property; (2) support for religion; and (3) community service and personal achievement. Another important element is the trust that individuals express in the government and political institutions. Unfortunately, trust in political institutions reached an all time low in 1992. Public opinion about the confidence in various institutions in our society has declined in the 1990s. Church and bank are lower than previous decades. The military and Supreme Court are the government institutions that have the highest levels of confidence. While the public may have little confidence in some government institutions, they still turn to government to solve major problems. While the exact influence of public opinion on government policy cannot be measured, it appears that politicians who ignore public opinion run a great risk of defeat in the next election.

Public Opinion: Why Is It Important Today?

Public opinion is a vital part of the political process. The over use of polls and poll results in the media seem to have caused a public reaction against this process. The sample of individuals willing to provide poll data is declining. This could be a dangerous trend, which makes it more difficult to accurately judge opinions on the serious issues affecting our society.

KEY TERMS

Agenda setting — p.195
consensus — p. 192
divisive opinion — p. 192
gender gap — p. 200
generational effect — p.196
media — p. 195
opinion leader — p. 195
opinion poll — p. 202

peer group — p. 194
political socialization — p. 193
political trust — p. 209
public opinion — p. 192
sampling error — p. 205
socioeconomic status — p. 196
Watergate break-in — p. 196

PRACTICE EXAM
[Answers appear at the end of this chapter.]

Fill-in-the-Blank. Supply the missing word(s) or term(s) to complete the sentence.

1. The aggregate of individual attitudes and beliefs is _____ _____.

2. How much people will express their opinions determines when private opinion becomes _____

    _____.

3. _____ _____ is polarized between two quite different positions.

4. One of the most common ways of gathering public opinion is _____ _____.

5. When a large proportion of the American public expresses the same view on an issue, we say that a _____ exists.

6. Roper, Gallup, and Crossley developed modern polling techniques to predict the total voting population by using _____ _____ with small samples of selected voters.

7. The most important principle in sampling public opinion is _____.

8. The _____ is the most important influence in political socialization.

9. _____ _____ is the term that describes the differences in issue orientation and voting behavior between men and women.

10. Determining which public policy questions will be debated or considered is called _____ _____.

True/False. Circle the appropriate letter to indicate if the statement is true or false.

T   F   1.   Adverse public opinion in 1968 caused President Johnson to decline to run for re-election.

T   F   2.   When public opinion is polarized between two quite different positions, we call it

                     _____ _____.

T   F   3.   The most important principle in sampling is randomness.

T   F   4.   Children accept their parents' political attitudes because of communication and receptivity.

T   F   5.   Education has little to do with interest or activity in politics.

T   F   6.   Most polls done via the Internet are accurate representations of public opinion.

T   F   7.   Family income is a strong predictor of economic liberalism or conservatism.

T   F   8.   The government institution the public has the most confidence in today is the military.

T   F   9.   Election research suggests that policymakers are responsive to public opinion.

T   F   10.   Well-defined public opinion tends to restrain government officials from taking unpopular actions.

Multiple-Choice. Circle the correct response.

1. The aggregate of individual attitudes or beliefs shared by some portion of adults is referred to as
    a. political opinion.
    b. propaganda.
    c. public opinion.
    d. an ideology.

2. General agreement among the citizenry on an issue is called
    a. propaganda.
    b. public opinion.
    c. consensus.
    d. political rhetoric

3. When public opinion is polarized between two quite different positions it is said to be
    a. consensus.
    b. divisive.
    c. private.
    d. in error.

4. The Literary Digest polling activities was an example of
    a. modern polling techniques.
    b. the use of exit interviews.
    c. a nonrepresentative sample.
    d. telephone interviews.

5. The most important principle in sampling is
    a. a large sample.
    b. picking an issue where consensus can be found.
    c. randomness.
    d. asking the right questions.

6. Sampling error is the difference between the sample result and the
    a. eligible voters.
    b. likely voters.
    c. true result.
    d. biased result.

7. Urban voters tend to
    a. split their votes pretty evenly between Democrats and Republicans.
    b. vote more heavily Republican.
    c. vote more heavily Democratic.
    d. vote at higher rates that rural and suburban voters.

8. Push polls are
    a. the most accurate opinion polls.
    b. used by candidates to influence voters.
    c. used by television reporters.
    d. like quota sampling.

9. The most important influence on political socialization is
    a. peer group.
    b. family.
    c. political events.
    d. education.

10. A person's place of residence seems to effect political attitudes, with big city dwellers tending to be
    a. liberal and Democratic.
    b. liberal and Republican.
    c. conservative and Democratic.
    d. conservative and Republican.

11. Independent voters make up _____ percent of all voters.
    a. 20
    b. 30
    c. 50
    d. 10

12. Fundamentalist or evangelical Christians tend to support
    a. Democrats.
    b. Republicans.
    c. Independents.
    d. no political parties at all.

13. Political events like the Vietnam War tend to produce what are called
    a. peer group influence.
    b. social and economic influence.
    c. opinion leader influence.
    d. generational effects.

14. According to studies, which group is mostly likely to use media to form basic political attitudes
    a. the elderly.
    b. college graduates.
    c. high school students.
    d. women.

15. The impact of strong public opinion on government action
    a. encourages officials to ignore public opinion.
    b. allows government officials to shape policy according to opinion polls.
    c. restrains officials from taking truly unpopular actions.
    d. discourages public officials from standing up for what is right.

16. The most important problem(s) facing the nation according to poll reports in 2004, was:
    a. morality.
    b. terrorism.
    c. war in Iraq and the economy.
    d. unemployment and crime.

17. The Gender Gap refers to voting in which women voted for
    a. Ronald Reagan.
    b. woman candidates.
    c. Republican presidential candidates.
    d. Democrat presidential candidates.

18. According to political scientists, Page and Shapiro, the government responds to public opinion about
    a. 10 percent of the time.
    b. 30 percent of the time.
    c. half (50 percent) of the time.
    d. two-thirds of the time.

19. Although people do not have much confidence in government institutions, polls show that they
    a. expect government to solve major problems.
    b. expect nonprofits to solve major problems.
    c. expect individuals to solve major problems by dropping out of society.
    d. avoid thinking about problems.

20. Which of the following statements about public opinion polls is correct?
    a. Public opinion polls lead to direct policy change.
    b. Public opinion polls do not identify issues important to the public.
    c. Public opinion polls are not very important in the political process today.
    d. Public opinion polls do identify issues important to the public.

Short Essay Questions. Briefly address the major concepts raised by the following questions.

1. Define the qualities of public opinion.

2. Describe the key factors in conducting opinion polls.

3. Explain the most important influences in political socialization.

4. Discuss the most important values of the American political system and the trends of political trust in the last three decades.

ANSWERS TO THE PRACTICE EXAM

Fill-in-the-Blank.

1. public opinion
2. public opinion
3. divisive opinion
4. opinion polls
5. consensus
6. personal interviews
7. randomness
8. family
9. gender gap
10. agenda setting

True/False.

1. T	3. T	5. F	7. T	9. T
2. T	4. T	6. F	8. T	10. T

Multiple Choice.

1. c	6. c	11. b	16. c
2. c	7. c	12. b	17. d
3. b	8. b	13. d	18. d
4. c	9. b	14. c	19. a
5. c	10. a	15. c	20. d

Short Essay Answers.

An adequate short answer consists of several paragraphs that discuss the concepts addressed by the question. Always demonstrate your knowledge of the ideas by giving examples. The following represent major ideas that should be included in these short essays.

1. Define public opinion.
   - The aggregate of individual attitudes or beliefs shared by some portion of the adult population.
   - Consensus opinion is general agreement among the citizenry on an issue.
   - Divisive opinion is public opinion that is polarized between two quite different positions.

2. Describe the key factors in conducting opinion polls. There are three key factors in conducting accurate public opinion polls.
   - Randomness is the most important factor. The sample to be interviewed must be representative of the whole population. One technique is to choose a random sample of telephone numbers. A quota sampling, which is not as accurate, is to select people who represent certain types of people. The major polls can interview about 1,500 people and predict elections within a margin of three percent, plus or minus.
   - Timing is a second factor. Polls continue to be conducted until the election day because a shift in opinion at the last minute can produce an unexpected outcome. The polls in the presidential election of 1980 between Carter and Reagan showed a very close contest. Reagan won easily, because of a shift in the undecided vote in the last week of the election.
   - The types of questions asked on the survey have a major impact on the results of the poll. If poorly worded or leading questions are asked, the result will be distorted.

3. Explain the most important influences in political socialization. Political socialization is the process by which individuals acquire political beliefs and attitudes.
   - The family is the most important influence and largely responsible for political party choice.
   - Schools are most likely to influence the understanding of issues and political activity.
   - Peer groups most strongly influence direct involvement in political activity.
   - Religion has some impact on political activity, but its influence is not clear.
   - Wealth and social-class influence a tolerance for differences and more voting activity.
   - Generational events, such as the great Depression, can influence opinion for decades.
   - Charismatic opinion leaders using the power of media can have a tremendous impact on opinion.
   - The demographic factors of age, gender, location, and region of residence have the final influences on the process we call political socialization.

4. Discuss the most important values of the American political system and the trend in political trust over the last three decades. The core elements of the American political system include:
   - Liberty, equality, and property.
   - Support for religion.
   - Community service and personal achievement.
   - These generally supported values provide an environment of support for the political system, which helps the system survive a crisis such as scandal. The levels of political trust that citizens have in the system declined tremendously in the 1960s and 1970s and reached an all-time low in 1992. The military and the Supreme Court are the most trusted parts of the political system today.

Chapter 7
INTEREST GROUPS

CHAPTER SUMMARY

The role of interest groups in the American political process can be illustrated by their activities with respect to legislation passed by Congress after the September 11 attacks on the World Trade Center and the Pentagon. In 2003, although there were mounting anti-war protests, most Americans supported President Bush in his policy of war against Iraq.

Interest Groups: A Natural Phenomenon

Pluralist theory, discussed in chapter 1, advocates that the structure of American government invites a political process in which interest groups compete with each other. Famed French visitor Alexis de Tocqueville observed in 1834 that America seemed to be a nation of joiners of associations. Interest groups are often created from mass social movements that represent the demands of a large segment of the population for major social change. The Civil Rights movement of the 1950s and 1960s is a good example of a social movement.

Why Do Americans Join Interest Groups?

According to the theory of Mancur Olson, it is not rational for individuals to join groups. If a group is successful in getting some benefit, how can that benefit be denied to others in the same situation? Why pay union dues if workers' benefits achieved by the union go to all workers? It is more logical to wait for others to gain benefits and then share them. People need incentives to join groups. The three major incentives are solidary, material, and purposive. Solidary incentives include companionship, a sense of belonging, and the pleasure of associating together. Material incentives are of course economic benefits or opportunities. Purposive incentives relate to ones ethical beliefs or ideological principles.

Types of Interest Groups

Although thousands of groups exist to influence government, they can be discussed in a few broad categories. A variety of economic interest groups mirror the complexity of the American economy and include business, agriculture, labor, public employee, and professional organizations. The largest business groups are the National Association of Manufactures (NAM), U.S. Chamber of Commerce, and the Business Roundtable. American farmers have been very successful lobbying for government support, even though they represent about 2 percent of U.S. workers. The American Farm Bureau and the National Farmers' Union are the most powerful agriculture groups. Labor unions have tired to balance the power of business groups but have weakened in recent years. The biggest union is the giant AFL-CIO. Public Employee interest groups have grown in recent years. These groups are similar to unions but lack the legal power to strike, which has not stopped them from strikes. One of the biggest of these unions is the American Federation of State, County, and Municipal Employees (AFSCME). Finally, professional occupations, such as lawyers and doctors are well represented in the American Bar Association and American Medical Association. Environmental interest groups actually began in the early part of the century, with the National Audubon Society and the Sierra Club. Mass memberships groups have been created since Earth Day in 1972. These groups include National Wildlife Federation and the Nature Conservancy. Public interest groups, concerned with the public good, have been created almost single-handedly by consumer activist Ralph Nader. Some of the largest public interest groups that have developed without Nader's help are Common Cause and the American Civil Liberties Union. Special interest groups, sometimes called single interest groups, can be very effective because they concentrate resources on a single issue. The National Rifle Association and the American Association of Retired Persons are good examples of this type of group. Finally, foreign governments of the largest trading partners of the U.S. hire lobbyists to try to influence trade policy. Japan, South Korea, Canada, and the European Union (EU) are just a few of the foreign government interest groups.

What Makes an Interest Group Powerful?

There are four factors that allow interest groups to attain a reputation for being powerful. These are the membership size, leadership, financial resources, and cohesiveness.

Interest Group Strategies

Interest group techniques of influence can be divided into direct techniques and indirect techniques. The direct techniques use lobbying, publicizing ratings of public officials, and campaign contributions. Lobbyists are private citizens who meet public officials on behalf of the interest that they represent. See page 238 for a list of lobbying activities. Many groups will publish the voting records of legislators on issues of interest to the group. Indirect techniques use the general public or individuals to influence the government for the interest group. Interest groups will try to generate a "groundswell" of support through mass mailing and advertising. Climate control is a similar concept, where organizations will use public relation techniques to try to create favorable public opinion about a group or industry. Another effective indirect technique is use constituents to lobby the lawmaker. The "shotgun" approach tries to get as many people as possible to write, call, or E-mail. In the "rifle" approach, the group tries to get a few influential constituents to talk to the lawmaker. A final indirect technique is to form an alliance with other groups that are concerned with the same legislation.

Regulating Lobbyists

The first attempt to regulate lobbyists and lobbying activities was the Legislative Reorganization Act of 1946. This law was ruled constitutional in the Supreme Court case of United States v. Harriss in 1954. The Court upheld a narrow interpretation of the law, which meant that very few lobbyists actually registered under the law. In 1995, Congress passed a far-reaching lobby regulation law, which should require three to ten times as many lobbyists to register. Congress also decided to change rules relating to gifts and travel expenses. See page 242-243 for a list of the major provisions of the law.

Interest Groups and Representative Democracy

The role of interest groups in our democracy is a continuing topic of debate. Clearly, members of interest groups are middle or upper class in background. Leaders of interest groups can be called an "elite within an elite" because often they are from a higher social class than the members of the group. Pluralist theory from chapter 1 presumes that groups compete with each other for the benefit of the members, but there is a very strong presence of elites in this picture, which is Elite theory from chapter 1. In the overall analysis of interest groups, it is clear that even the most powerful group does not always prevail. By definition, an interest group can only be effective on a narrow range of interests that hold the group together. When groups try to deal with broad policy issues, they fragment their membership base and cannot influence policy.

Interest Groups: Why Are They Important Today?

The role of interest groups in American society has been debated since the writing of the Constitution. James Madison warned us in the Federalists Papers about the "spirit of faction." The debate for the future seems to be focused on the issue of campaign contributions by interest groups. One possible solution is public financing, which is used in the Presidential election. Groups will continue to prosper in the future, as they provide real opportunities for more and more citizens to participate in the political process and to influence public policy toward their interest.

KEY TERMS

Boycott — p. 241
Climate control — p. 240
Direct technique — p. 238
Free rider problem — p. 224
Indirect technique — p. 238
Interest group — p. 221
Labor movement — p. 228
Latent interests — p. 224

Lobbyist — p. 221
Material incentive — p. 225
Public interest — p. 233
Purposive incentive — p. 226
Service sector — p. 229
Social movement — p. 223
Solidary incentive — p. 225

PRACTICE EXAM
(Answers appear at the end of this chapter.)

Fill-in-the-Blank. Supply the missing word(s) or term to complete the sentence.

1. An interest group must give individuals a _____ to become members.

2. _____ _____ represent the demands of a large segment of the public for social change.

3. Numerous interest groups in the United States have been formed to promote _____ interests.

4. In spite of representing about 2% of the population, _____ interest groups have been very successful in receiving government aid.

5. Since 1965, the degree of unionization of the _____ sector has declined, but this has been offset by the growth of unionization of _____ employees.

6. Consumer activist _____ _____ has organized the most well known public interest groups.

7. The nation's largest interest group is the _____ _____ _____ _____.

8. The techniques used by interest groups may be divided into those that are _____ and _____.

9. More interest groups are formed to represent _____ interests than any other set of interests.

10. _____ _____ is a public relations strategy by an interest group to improve its public image.

True/False. Circle the appropriate letter to indicate if the statement is true or false.

T F 1. The structure of our political system makes it difficult for individuals and groups to exert influence on the system.

T F 2. James Madison was a firm believer in strengthening interest group activity.

T F 3. The strength of union membership has traditionally been in the service sector of the workforce.

T F 4. Foreign governments are prohibited from lobbying in the United States.

T F 5. The use of public relations techniques to influence public opinion about a group is called the rifle approach.

T F 6. Solidary incentives include a sense of belonging, companionship, and the pleasure of associating with others.

T F 7. One of the most effective interest group activities is the use of constituents to lobby for the group's goals.

T F 8. Most interest groups have a middle-class or upper-class bias.

T F 9. Today, the power of interest groups is on the wane.

T F 10. The existence of interest groups allows individuals to influence government far beyond just voting.

Multiple Choice. Circle the correct response.

1. Any organized group whose members share common objectives and actively attempt to influence the government is a(n)
    a. political party.
    b. bureaucracy.
    c. interest group.
    d. institution.

2. It is possible for individuals and groups to exert influence at many different points in our government because
    a. officials are always looking for campaign contributions.
    b. interest group members are also voters.
    c. of the structure of our political system.
    d. we have a unitary form of government.

3. Companionship, a sense of belonging, and the pleasure of associating with others as reasons for belonging to interest groups are referred to as
    a. material incentives.
    b. purposive incentives.
    c. solidary incentives.
    d. herd incentives.

4. Interest groups are often spawned by mass
    a. increases of young voters.
    b. publication of "underground" newspapers.
    c. factionalism.
    d. social movements.

5. The role of labor unions in American society has weakened in recent years, as witnessed by
    a. the rise of business groups.
    b. a decline in union membership.
    c. the lack of effective leadership.
    d. an increase in government regulation.

6. Since 1965, the greatest growth in unionization has occurred in the unionization of
    a. military personnel.
    b. professional athletes.
    c. public employees.
    d. private sector employees.

7. Lobbying, ratings of legislative behavior, and campaign assistance are
    a. the main indirect techniques used by interest groups.
    b. considered ineffective methods of swaying votes.
    c. the main direct techniques used by interest groups.
    d. considered obsolete in view of today's modern technology.

8. One of the largest public interest groups is
    a. Institute for Justice.
    b. NAACP.
    c. AARP.
    d. Common Cause.

9. The U.S. v Harris case ruled that the Federal Regulation of Lobbying Act
   a. is constitutional.
   b. is unconstitutional.
   c. should be left to the states to regulate.
   d. only applies to presidential elections.

10. The "shotgun" approach to lobbying consists of
    a. mobilizing large numbers of constituents to write or phone their legislators.
    b. identifying specific constituents to write or phone their legislators.
    c. concentrating only on gun control issues.
    d. allowing lobbyists to determine the most appropriate strategy.

11. One of the benefits of forming alliances between interest groups is that
    a. it is easier to keep track of interest groups if they are fewer in numbers.
    b. it makes it easier to solicit contributions.
    c. there is strength in numbers.
    d. it shares expenses and multiplies the influence.

12. Which of the following is NOT something that makes interest groups powerful?
    a. size
    b. ability to offer the most solidary resources
    c. leadership
    d. resources

13. Interest groups tend to have a(n)
    a. lower class bias.
    b. middle to upper-class bias.
    c. a neutral bias.
    d. a democratic foundation for decision-making.

14. The nation's largest interest group is the
    a. American Association of Retired Persons.
    b. Common Cause.
    c. National Education Association.
    d. National Rifle Association.

15. The great advantage for democracy in interest group activity is that
    a. it is a way to demonstrate support for governmental policy.
    b. individual citizens are empowered to influence government.
    c. it serves as a basis of political party organization.
    d. it is a way to monitor the activities of Congress.

16. Which of the following is not a special one-issue interest group?
    a. National Abortion Rights
    b. National Rifle Association
    c. The Right to Work Committee
    d. AFL-CIO

17. Foreign governments are
    a. banned by the Constitution from lobbying in the U.S.
    b. banned by Congress from lobbying in the U.S.
    c. able to lobby extensively.
    d. able to lobby, but rarely do so.

18. The use of public-relation techniques to create favorable public opinion toward an interest group is called
    a. lobbying.
    b. rating.
    c. climate control.
    d. groundswell.

19. The theory that views politics as a struggle among interest groups is
    a. elitism.
    b. democracy.
    c. pluralism.
    d. federalism.

20. The "founding father" who worried about how to control the "mischiefs of faction" was
    a. Thomas Jefferson.
    b. James Madison.
    c. George Washington.
    d. John Adams.

Short Essay Questions. Briefly address the major concepts raised by the following questions.

1. Discuss the incentives for an individual to join an interest group.

2. Describe the various types of major interest groups.

3. Explain the direct techniques used by interest groups to influence government.

4. Discuss the indirect techniques used by interest groups to influence government.

ANSWERS TO THE PRACTICE EXAM

Fill-in-the-blank.

1. incentive
2. social movements
3. economic
4. agricultural
5. private, public
6. Ralph Nader
7. American Association of Retired Persons
8. direct, indirect
9. economic
10. climate control

True/False.

1. F	3. F	5. F	7. T	9. F
2. T	4. F	6. T	8. T	10. T

Multiple Choice.

1. c	6. c	11. d	16. d
2. c	7. c	12. b	17. c
3. c	8. d	13. b	18. c
4. d	9. a	14. a [	19. c
5. b	10. a	15. b	20. b

Short Essay.

An adequate short answer consists of several paragraphs that relate to concepts addressed by the question. Always demonstrate your knowledge of the ideas by giving examples. The following represent major ideas that should be included in the short essay answer.

1. Discuss the incentives for an individual to join an interest group.
   - There are three major incentives for individuals to join interest groups: solidary, material, and purposive.
     - Solidary incentives include companionship, a sense of belonging, and the pleasure of associating with others.
     - Material incentives are economic benefits or opportunities, such as discounts, insurance, or travel planning.
     - Purposive incentives provide the satisfaction of taking action for one's beliefs or principles.

2. Describe the various types of major interest groups.
   - The major types of interest groups are economic, environmental, public, special, and foreign governments.
     - Economic interest groups include business, agricultural, labor, public employees, and professional.
     - Environmental interest groups began in 1905 with the National Audubon society. More recent groups include the National Wildlife Federation and the Nature Conservancy.
     - Public interest groups were greatly influenced by consumer activist Ralph Nader. One of the largest public interest groups today is Common Cause.
     - Special interest groups, or single-interest groups, focus on one issue such as for and against abortion or gun control.
     - Foreign governments that are major trading partners of the U.S. lobby for trade concessions and aid from the U.S. government.

3. Explain the direct techniques used by interest groups to influence government.
   - There are three important direct techniques of interest group influence. These are lobbying, rating of legislators, and campaign assistance.
     - Lobbying entails a range of activities, which include private meetings, testifying in public meetings, drafting legislation, providing political information, and influencing during social occasions.
     - Rating of legislators on specific votes on issues important to the group provides the members of the group with important information on which candidates to vote for.
     - Campaign assistance in the form of campaign contribution has grown tremendously in the past two decades because of the increase in the number of Political Action Committees (PAC). PACs account for about one-third of all campaign contributions.

4. Discuss the indirect techniques used by interest groups to influence government.
   - Indirect techniques allow interest groups to influence government policy by using the general public, individual constituents, and other interest groups.
     - Interest groups try to create a "groundswell" of public opinion by using mass advertising. Sometimes, public relations techniques are used to create favorable public opinion toward the interest. This technique is known as climate control.
     - The use of individual constituents is one of the most successful techniques. The attempt to mobilize as many constituents as possible is know as the "shotgun" approach. An attempt to mobilize very influential constituents is called the "rifle" approach.
     - Building an alliance with other interest groups on common issues allows groups to share costs and multiply their influence.

Chapter 8
POLITICAL PARTIES

CHAPTER SUMMARY

What is a Political Party?
A political party is a group of political activists who organize to win elections, to operate the government, and to determine public policy. A faction is a group that acts together in pursuit of some special interest.

Function of Political Parties in the United States
Political parties have five basic functions. These are: (1) recruiting candidates for public office, (2) organizing and running elections, (3) presenting alternative policies, (4) accepting responsibility for operating the government, and (5) acting as the organized opposition to the party in power.

A Short History of Political Parties in the United States
The evolution of our political party system can be divided into six periods. The first period from 1789 to 1812 was the creation of political parties. The Federalists pushed for adoption of the Constitution, and the Anti-Federalists were against adoption. The second period from 1816 to 1824 was the era of personal politics because elections centered on individual candidates rather than parties. The third period of Andrew Jackson's presidency to the Civil War, from 1828-1860, saw the birth and death of the Whig party. The fourth period from 1864 to 1892 was the creation of the heavily Democratic South and the heavily Republican North. The next period from 1896 to 1928 saw the development of the Progressive Party, which ran Theodore Roosevelt for President in 1912. The final period was the modern era from 1932 to the present. The new deal of President Franklin Roosevelt created the basic landscape of politics that we have today.

The Two Major U.S. Parties and their Members
The core of the Democratic Party is minorities, the working class, and various ethnic groups. Democrats generally support government intervention in the economy to help individuals in need. The Republican Party draws its support from college graduates, upper-income families, and professionals or businesspersons. Republicans support the private marketplace and feel that the government should be involved in fewer social programs.

The Three Faces of a Party
Each political party consists of three major components. These are the party-in-the-electorate, which are people who express a preference for one party over the other; the party organization, which are structure, staff, and official members of the party; and the party-in-government, who are the elected and appointed government officials.

Party Organization
American political parties have a standard, pyramid-shaped organization. The national party organization consists of the national convention, which selects the national committee, and national chairperson to direct the party during the four-year period between the national conventions. The state party organization consists of a state committee, state chairperson, and a number of local organizations. States parties are important in national politics because of the unit rule, which allots electoral votes in an indivisible bloc except in Maine and Nebraska. The lowest level of party organization, called the grass roots, is composed of county and district party officials, precinct chairpersons, and party workers. The political machine no longer exists because of the decline of patronage. Local political organization can still have a major impact on elections, particularly local elections.

Why Has the Two-Party System Endured?
There are a number of factors that explain why the United States has a two-party system. The historical development of political parties in the Federalists and Anti-Federalists laid the foundation for two parties based on two distinct sets of interests. Political socialization of children to identify with the party of the parent has been an important factor in maintaining the two-party system, which was already established. The political

culture has been one of consensus and moderation. This has helped to maintain the two-party system. The winner-take-all election system, particularly the Electoral College for electing the President, makes it very difficult for third parties to have any electoral success. Finally, most state and federal election laws provide a clear advantage to the two major parties. Third party candidates for President are not eligible for federal matching funds.

The Role of Minor Parties in U.S. Political History

Minor parties have not been able to compete very successfully with the two major parties but have played an important role in our political life. Ideological based minor parties, such as the Socialist Party, remain active today and had real electoral success in the early twentieth century. The most successful minor parties split from the major parties. The Bull Moose Progressive Party in 1912 nominated Theodore Roosevelt for President, which created a three-way race, and gave the election to the Democrat Woodrow Wilson. A Democrat splinter party, the American Independent Party, supported George Wallace for President in 1968, and he did receive 46 electoral votes for President, but this did not seem to affect the outcome of Richard Nixon's victory. Other minor parties, which include the Greenback and Populists, have appeared for specific economic issues and then disappeared fairly quickly. Minor parties have had an impact on American politics by raising important political issues, which are usually taken over by the two major parties, and in some cases determining the outcome of the presidential election. The third party candidate in 1992, H. Ross Perot, probably took votes away from Republican George Bush to give the victory to Democrat Bill Clinton.

The Uncertain Future of Party Identification

The current state of political party identification seems to indicate a movement away from the two major parties. Thirty-four percent of voters today classify themselves as independents.

Mechanisms of Political Change

Do voters switch parties? What impact does this switching have? This section discusses the role of realignment, dealignment, and tipping.

Political Parties: Why Are They Important Today?

American political parties face a number of challenges for the future. Parties must address the issues of what they offer to the voters, what to do about independent candidates that can fund their own campaign or form their own political party, and the dilemma of, do the major parties actually stand for different positions on the issues?

KEY TERMS

Dealignment — p. 278
Democratic Party — p. 254
Divided government — p. 268
Electoral College — p. 277
Era of good feelings — p. 254
Faction — p. 251
Independent — p. 251
National committee — p. 264
National convention — p. 263
Party identification — p. 278
Party-in-government — p. 263
Party-in-the-electorate — p. 262
Party organization — p. 263
Party platform — p. 263
Patronage — p. 266
Plurality — p. 270

Political party — p. 251
Realignment — p. 277
Republican party — p. 254
Reverse-income effect — p. 262
Safe seat — p. 269
Splinter party — p. 273
State central committee — p. 266
Straight ticket voting — p. 279
Swing voters — p. 279
Third party — p. 271
Ticket-splitting — p. 268
Two-party system — p. 252
Unit rule — p. 266
Whig Party — p. 254

PRACTICE EXAM
(Answers appear at the end of this chapter.)

Fill-in-the-Blank. Supply the missing word(s) or term to complete the sentence.

1. A _____ _____ is a group of individuals who organize to win elections, to operate the government, and to determine public policy.

2. The first _____ political division in the United States occurred prior to the adoption of the Constitution.

3. The _____ Party is the oldest continuing political party in the western world.

4. The major political American political party, which emerged in the late 1850s from the remains of the Whig Party, was the _____ _____.

5. The structure of U.S. political parties is largely autonomous, reflecting a _____ structure.

6. The _____ _____ _____ is responsible for carrying out policy decisions of the party's state convention.

7. The national chairperson of the party is selected during the _____ _____.

8. In 1884, Protestant minister Samuel Burchard described the _____ Party as the party of "rum, Romanism, and rebellion."

9. In the 36 years between 1968 and 2004, there were only _____ years when one of the two major parties controlled the presidency, the House, and the Senate.

10. Most minor parties that have endured have had a strong _____ foundation.

True/False. Circle the appropriate letter to indicate if the statement is true or false.

T	F	1.	Party-in-the-Electorate is those members of the general public who express a preference for one party over another.
T	F	2.	American political parties are tightly organized pyramid-shaped organizations with the national chairperson dictating policy to lower levels.
T	F	3.	The party platform is largely ignored once one of the two major parties captures control of the government.
T	F	4.	The national chairperson for the two major parties is actually chosen by their respective party's presidential nominee.
T	F	5.	The Libertarian party advocates federal regulation of industry to protect consumers, workers, and small businesses.
T	F	6.	In a plurality system, the winner is the one who gets the most votes.
T	F	7.	Virtually all levels of government in the United States use the plurality, winner-take-all electoral system.
T	F	8.	The Green Party may have had an impact on the 2000 presidential election.
T	F	9.	Minor parties have not played an important role in American politics.
T	F	10.	Tipping refers to a phenomenon in which one group grows large enough to tip the balance in a state to the opposing party.

Multiple Choice. Circle the correct response.

1. The main feature differentiating a faction from a political party is that a faction
    a. is composed only of conservatives, while a political party may have both liberals and conservatives.
    b. generally does not have a permanent organized structure.
    c. works best if there are competing factions in opposition to it.
    d. helps to extend democracy to the rank-and-file party member.

2. Political parties in the United States tend to perform all of the following activities except
    a. recruit candidates for public office.
    b. organize and run elections.
    c. act as the organized opposition to the party in power.
    d. establish a large cadre of highly disciplined dues-paying party members.

3. The first two opposing groups in United States politics were the
    a. Democrats and Republicans.
    b. Federalists and Anti-Federalists.
    c. Washingtonians and Jeffersonians.
    d. Independents and Whigs.

4. The era from 1816 to 1828 when attention was centered on the character of the individual running for office rather than on party identification is referred to as
    a. the era of good feeling.
    b. factional politics.
    c. personal politics.
    d. democratic politics.

5. After the end of the Civil, the _____ became heavily Democratic, and the _____ became heavily Republican.
    a. North-South
    b. South-North
    c. East-West
    d. West-East

6. The modern party system was created from the
    a. Post-Civil War period.
    b. Progressive Movement.
    c. New Deal period.
    d. Vietnam protest period.

7. The main purpose of the national party conventions every four years is to
    a. nominate the presidential and vice-presidential candidates.
    b. write a party platform.
    c. check the credentials of all party activists.
    d. develop a strategy for the upcoming presidential election.

8. A situation in which one major party controls the presidency and the other controls Congress is referred to as
    a. ticket splitting.
    b. divided government.
    c. party division.
    d. federalism.

9. The principal organized structure within states for each political party is the
    a. precinct committee.
    b. ward captain.
    c. state central committee.
    d. governor's council.

10. Rewarding members of a political party with government jobs and/or contracts is known as
    a. bribery.
    b. graft and corruption.
    c. non-competitive bidding.
    d. patronage.

11. Since the presidency of Franklin D. Roosevelt, the core of the Democratic Party has been
    a. middle-class, working Americans.
    b. upper-class liberals.
    c. minorities, the working class and ethnic groups.
    d. middle to upper-class protestants and independents.

12. In the early 1900s, a spirit of political reforms arose in both parties called
    a. libertarianism.
    b. sectionalism.
    c. progressivism.
    d. reformism.

13. Historically, the major division in American politics has been over _____ issues.
    a. religious
    b. social
    c. foreign policy
    d. economic

14. The longest lived minor parties
    a. are those which split from a major party.
    b. are those with strong ideological foundations.
    c. are those focused on the positive, not negative.
    d. are those opposed to existing major parties.

15. Which of the following statement about party identification is true?
    a. In recent years, Democrats have increased, while Republicans and Independents have decreased.
    b. In recent years, Independents have increased, while Democrats and Republicans have decreased.
    c. In recent years, Republicans have increased, while Democrats and Independents have decreased.
    d. In recent years, Democrats, Republicans, and Independents have decreased.

16. The most important reason for the creation of splinter parties is
    a. ideology.
    b. class politics.
    c. a particular political personality.
    d. the U.S. political culture.

17. The third party which may have cost Democrat Al Gore the presidency in the 2000 election was the
    a. Green Party.
    b. Reform Party.
    c. Socialist Party.
    d. Libertarian Party.

18. Independent voters in the 2000 presidential election, composed _____ percent of the electorate.
    a. 33
    b. 40
    c. 50
    d. 55

19. Calling the U.S. a two-party system is an oversimplification because
    a. a third party candidate almost won the 2000 presidential election.
    b. the nature and names of the two major parties have changed over time.
    c. ideology is such an important factor in U.S. elections.
    d. third parties receive equal public funding with major parties.

20. The best indication that political parties have weakened in the last three decades is
    a. low voter turnout.
    b. low party identification.
    c. high numbers of PACs.
    d. the lack of media coverage.

Short Essay Questions. Briefly address the major concepts raised by the following questions.

1. Distinguish between a political party, interest group, and faction.

2. Trace the evolution of political party development within the United States.

3. Identify the formal structure of political party organization in America.

4. Discuss the reasons for the two-party system in the United States.

ANSWERS TO THE PRACTICE EXAM

Fill-in-the-blank.

1. political party
2. partisan
3. Democratic
4. Republican Party
5. confederal
6. state central committee
7. national convention
8. Democratic
9. eight
10. ideological

True/False.

1. T	3. F	5. F	7. T	9. F
2. F	4. T	6. T	8. T	10. T

Multiple Choice.

1. b	6. c	11. c	16. c
2. d	7. a	12. c	17. a
3. b	8. b	13. d	18. a
4. c	9. c	14. b	19. b
5. b	10. d	15. b	20. b

Short Essay Questions. Briefly address the major concepts raised by the following questions.

1. Distinguish between a political party, interest group, and faction.
    *   A political party is a group of political activists who organize to win elections, to operate the government, and to determine public policy.
    *   An interest group is a collection of individuals that attempt to influence elections, influence the elected officials, and to influence public policy.
    *   Factions are smaller groups, which may exist within political parties, and are trying to obtain certain benefits for themselves.

2. Trace the evolution of political party development within the United States.
    *   The formation of political parties in the U.S. went through six basic periods. These are: (1) the creation of parties, (2) the era of personal politics, (3) the period of President Jackson to the Civil War, (4), the post-Civil War period, (5) the progressive period, and (6) the modern period.
        *   The first parties were created from 1789 to 1812 around support for ratifying the Constitution, the Federalists, or against ratification, the Anti-Federalists.
        *   From 1816 to 1828, voters focused on the candidates rather than the parties.
        *   From 1828 to 1860, political parties tended to focus on Andrew Jackson, and the Democratic and Whig parties developed.
        *   The post-Civil War period of 1864 to 1892 created our current two-party system, as the anti-slavery Republican Party was created.
        *   The Progressive era from 1896 to 1928 led to the split in the Republican Party and the election of the Democrats in 1912, which enacting much of the Progressive Party platform.
        *   The New Deal programs of President Franklin Roosevelt, which established the current political landscape of the political party system, created the modern period from 1932.

3. Identify the formal structure of political party organization in America.
    *   The formal political party organization structure consists of the national level, the state level, and the local level.
        *   The national party organization consists of a national convention, held every four years. At this convention, the party selects its candidates for president and vice president, writes a party platform, selects a national committee, and selects a national chairperson.
        *   The state central committee will carry out the decisions of the state party convention and in some states direct the activities of the state chairperson.
        *   The local party organization called the grass roots uses county committees and their chairperson to direct and assist the activities of precinct leaders.

4. Discuss the reasons for the two-party system in the United States.
    *   The historical foundations of the two-party system developed around relatively distinct sets of issues.
    *   The first of these issues were ratifying the Constitution, which led to the Federalists and Anti-Federalists.
    *   Political socialization in which parents influence their children's choice of political party continued the two-party system.
    *   The American political culture emphasizes the commonality of goals, which makes the two party broad and able to accommodate different viewpoints.
    *   The winner-take-all election system makes it very difficult for third parties to win elections.
    *   State and federal election laws make it difficult for third parties to get on the ballot.

Chapter 9
Campaigns, Elections, and the Media

CHAPTER SUMMARY

The People Who Run for Political Office
People who run for political office can be divided into two groups: those who are "self-starters," and those who are recruited. There are few constitutional requirements to run for federal office. For President, a candidate must be a natural-born citizen, age 35, and a resident of the U.S. for fourteen years when sworn in. For Vice President, the same requirements as President, and cannot be a resident of the same state as the President. For Senator, a citizen for nine years, 30 years old, and a resident of the state in which he/she is elected. For Representative, a citizen for seven years, 25 years old, and a resident of the state in which he/she is elected. While these requirements are minimal, most current office holders are white males. This is largely because of past discrimination, and women for one group, have made tremendous gains in elected officials in the last 10 years. See Figure 9-1 page 291, for a look at the number of women candidates and representatives elected. Most candidates elected to office tend to be professionals, especially lawyers.

The Twenty-First Century Campaign
American political campaigns are extravagant yearlong events that cost a total of several billion dollars in 2004. As was noted in chapter 8, fewer people are identifying with political parties now, which means that campaigns are changing and candidates have to spend more money to get out the vote with paid staff. Most candidates, since the 1960s, will hire a professional paid political consultant to run the campaign.

The Strategy of Winning
The goal of every political campaign is to win the election. One of the most important concerns is how known the candidate is. The problem of name recognition is obviously a problem for a third party candidate because they do not have the well-known Democrat or Republican name to run on. Most candidates will use two major strategies in the campaign, polls, and focus groups. Polls give the candidate information, and as the election approaches, tracking polls indicate how well the campaign is going. Focus groups allow the candidate to gain insights into the public's perception of the candidate.

Financing the Campaign
The tremendous cost of political campaigns has caused a lot of concern among the public and led Congress to pass a number of laws to attempt to regulate campaign financing. Beginning in 1925, the Corrupt Practices Acts were passed but proved largely ineffective. The Hatch Act in 1939 attempted to limit spending by political groups, but it was also easily evaded. The Federal Election Campaign Act of 1972 and 1974 essentially replaced all past laws and instituted a major reform. These laws created the Federal Election Commission (FEC), provided public funding for presidential elections, put limits on presidential spending, limited campaign contributions, and required disclosure by candidates. Within a few years of these laws, three major loopholes appeared. Soft money, given to political parties; independent expenditures is money to help a candidate but not part of his campaign; and bundling, adding together maximum contributions to influence a candidate, were all used to evade the new campaign financing laws. The Bipartisan Campaign Reform Act of 2002 bans soft money. How effective this law will be remains to be seen.

Running for President: The Longest Campaign
The American presidential election has two distinct phases. The first begins in January with the first presidential primary and end in June with the party's national convention. The second phase usually begins on Labor Day and culminates in the presidential election in November. After the riots at the 1968 Democratic National Convention caused major changes in the primary election system, presidential candidates realized that the primary elections could be a springboard to win the presidency. If a candidate wins the first caucus in Iowa and the first primary in New Hampshire, they will be labeled a front-runner by the media and receive a big boost in their campaign. Other states, attempting to get the media coverage and influence in the presidential nomination, began to move up the day of their primary elections.

A number of southern states moved their primaries to the same day, which became known as Super Tuesday. This practice of moving up the date of a presidential primary is known as front-loading. The national convention is the end result of all the state primary elections. In recent years, the delegates selected in the primaries have already given the nomination to a candidate before the convention begins. This has lessened the interest and media coverage of the national convention.

The Electoral College
The Constitution has created the Electoral College as the official method for electing the President. Each state is responsible for selecting electors who will officially vote for president. These electors are based on the number of Senators and Representatives that a state has. The total number of electors is 538. If a plurality of voters in a state chooses one slate of electors, then those electors are pledged to vote on the first Monday after the second Wednesday in December in the state capital for the president and vice president. The ballots are counted and certified before a joint session of Congress early in January. It requires 270 electoral votes to be elected president. This process has been criticized for a number of reasons, including the possibility that a candidate could win the popular vote but lose the electoral vote. The states with small electoral votes are ignored in the presidential campaign but do get more electoral votes for fewer people. The major reforms of the system which have been suggested are to have direct election of the president and to require electors to vote for the candidate that has a plurality in the state.

How Are Elections Conducted?
The United States uses the secret or Australian ballot for elections, which is prepared, distributed, and counted by government officials at public expense. There are two types of ballots: the office-block, which focuses on the office rather than the party, and the party-column, which focuses on the party rather than the office. In recent years, registering and voting have been available through the mail. Experts are divided over whether voting by mail increases participation or only increase the opportunity for fraud.

Voting in National, State, and Local Elections
Voting turnout in the United States in the 2004 presidential election was only 55.3 percent of voting-age population. There are two theories about the decline of voting turnout in the U.S. One is that the decline in voting turnout is a threat to our democracy. The other is that people are basically satisfied with the status quo, and that is why they don't vote. Studies show that there are a number of factors that seem to influence voting turnout. These factors are age, education, minority status, income, and two-party competition. Voters tend to be older, more educated, not minorities, wealthy, and where there is two-party competition. Political scientists believe that people don't vote because of a political withdrawal since 1960 and the rational ignorance effect, in which people chose not find out about issues because they believe their vote will not make a difference.

Legal Restrictions on Voting
Historically only white males who owned property were allowed to vote. The Constitution allowed the states to decide who should vote. Since the Civil War, Constitutional Amendments, and act of Congress, such as the Voting Rights Act, have extended the right to vote. Voting requires registration, and some scholars believe that even the minimal requirements of citizenship, age, and residency keep some people from voting.

The Media and Politics
This section discusses the role of the media in entertainment, reporting the news, identifying public problems, socializing new generations, providing a political forum, and making profits. It discusses the primacy of television as the most influential medium. The role of media in political campaigns is discussed, including the role of advertising, news coverage, presidential debate, and media impact on voters.

Campaigns, Nominations, and Elections: Why Are They Important Today?
The length and cost of political campaigns will continue to be issues of concern. The most pressing issue for the future seems to be the increasingly level of cynicism of voters, which may be a major factor in the low levels of participation at all governmental elections.

KEY TERMS

PRACTICE EXAM
(Answers appear at the end of this chapter.)

Fill-in-the-Blank. Supply the missing word(s) or term to complete the sentence.

1. In terms of characteristics, holders of political office in the U.S. are overwhelmingly _____and _____.

2. Candidates who run for office are described as "self-starters" and _____.

3. In the last three decades, campaigns have changed from volunteer campaign managers to paid _____ _____.

4. Campaign contributions banned by the Bipartisan Campaign Act of 2002 are referred to as _____ _____.

5. Today, candidates use focus groups and _____ _____ to find out how the campaign is going.

6. Each state's number of electors in the Electoral College equals to the state's number of _____ plus its number of _____ in the U.S. Congress.

7. A _____ _____ is a form of general election ballot in which the candidates are arranged in one column under their respective party name and symbol.

8. The mass media performs many different functions including _____ _____ , the primary function of the mass media.

9. An interpretation of campaign events or election results that is favorable to the candidate's campaign strategy is known as _____.

10. Many media outlets today are owned by a few _____ _____.

True/False. Circle the appropriate letter to indicate if the statement is true or false.

T   F   1. Today, when campaigning for public office, candidates are depending more and more upon the resources of political parties.

T   F   2. For the most part, media outlets depend on advertisers to make profits.

T   F   3.   Tracking polls are used by the government to keep track of campaign contributions.

T   F   4.   The purpose of instituting the primary election was to open the nomination process to ordinary party members.

T   F   5.   States began to change the dates of primaries to have more influence in nominating presidential candidates in a process known as front-loading.

T   F   6.   The framers of the constitution favored the selection of the president and vice president by the masses.

T   F   7.   In general, the more education you have the more likely you are to vote.

T   F   8.   In the case Buckley v. Valeo, the Supreme Court ruled it was unconstitutional to restrict in any way the amount congressional candidates could spend on their own behalf.

T   F   9.   Advocacy ads argue for or against a policy or an issue and are another form of political advertising.

T   F   10. In many states, prisoners once convicted of a felony are forever denied the right to vote.

Multiple Choice. Circle the correct response.

1.   The constitutional qualifications for the office of president include all of the following EXCEPT
     a.   natural born citizen
     b.   35 years of age
     c.   14-year resident of U.S.
     d.   registered voter.

2.   Which of the following characteristics is not descriptive of a professional campaign?
     a.   Increased length of campaign.
     b.   Paid political consultant.
     c.   Increased costs of campaign.
     d.   Increased use of volunteers.

3.   The first attempt by Congress to regulate campaign spending was the
     a.   Hatch Act.
     b.   Corrupt Practices Acts.
     c.   CREEP Act.
     d.   Federal Election Campaign Act.

4.   The purpose of the Federal Election Commission is to
     a.   create an aura of good feeling in federal elections.
     b.   oversee and enforce the provisions of the 1974 Federal Election Campaign Act.
     c.   scrutinize and attempt to discover loopholes in the 1974 Act.
     d.   oversee federal and state elections.

5.   The group that now controls the nomination process for president is the
     a.   mass public.
     b.   party elites.
     c.   presidential nominees themselves.
     d.   mass media.

6.   The framers of the constitution established the Electoral College because they wanted
     a.   to ensure the general population would have an opportunity to directly vote for president.
     b.   the choice of president and vice-president to be made by a few dispassionate, reasonable men.
     c.   only candidates for president and vice-president who had graduated from the Electoral College.
     d.   the political parties to be able to control the selection of president and vice-president.

7. The major parties are not in favor of eliminating the Electoral College because
    a. the electors are always influential party members who might be offended.
    b. the major party candidates would not receive as much public funding.
    c. the masses are not capable of making this important decision.
    d. they fear it would give minor parties a more influential role in the election outcome.

8. The form of ballot that encourages straight-ticket voting is the
    a. closed ballot.
    b. open ballot.
    c. office-block ballot.
    d. party-column ballot.

9. The coattail effect
    a. is only in national elections.
    b. refers to voting by mail.
    c. is the influence of the candidate that is at the top of the ballot.
    d. is an aspect of voter fraud.

10. Which statement is correct with respect to age as a factor in voting?
    a. Age is not a significant factor in voting.
    b. Younger voters tend to turn out in higher percentages than older voters.
    c. Turnout increases the older the age groups until the age of 65 and older.
    d. Younger voters have more enthusiasm for voting than older voters.

11. As a factor in voting, more education seems to be correlated with
    a. voting Republican.
    b. voting Democratic.
    c. voting independent.
    d. disillusionment and apathy.

12. Since their introduction in the late nineteenth century, voter registration laws have
    a. increased the numbers of voters.
    b. reduced the voting of African Americans and immigrants.
    c. created a new class of active and committed voters.
    d. allowed the manipulation of election results by party bosses.

13. Which of the following functions of the mass media is considered the primary function?
    a. Socializing new generations
    b. Making profits
    c. Entertainment
    d. Reporting the news

14. Using political advertising to get a message across to the public is
    a. regulated by the 1971 FECA.
    b. free but requires a good deal of time and skill.
    c. very expensive.
    d. prohibited by the 2002 FCC rulings.

15. Female candidates for the U.S. Senate totaled
    a. 13 in 2002.
    b. 7 in 2004.
    c. 2 in 1990.
    d. 8 in 2000.

16.   Which of the following is a provision of the Bipartisan Campaign Reform Act of 2002?
        a.   bans all soft-money contributions
        b.   bans all outside special interest ads
        c.   limits individual contributions to $1,000 per individual
        d.   bans only soft-money contribution to national political parties

17.   Front-Loading of presidential primaries refers to the practice of
        a.   spending massive sums of money on the first primary.
        b.   being the first candidate to announce a campaign for the presidency.
        c.   moving presidential primary elections to the early part of the campaign.
        d.   using the national convention to select the candidate.

18.   In 2000, Katherine Harris, Florida's top election official
        a.   served as Bush's campaign co-chair.
        b.   served as Gore's campaign co-chair.
        c.   was indicted for election fraud.
        d.   was elected to Congress.

19.   Which of the following measures to improve voter turnout have not been tried?
        a.   mail-in voting
        b.   registering when you apply for a driver's license
        c.   absentee voting
        d.   declaring election day a national holiday

20.   Extension of the franchise to black males occurred with the passage of the _____ amendment in 1870.
        a.   14th
        b.   15th
        c.   16th
        d.   21st

Short Essay Questions. Briefly address the major concepts raised by the following questions.

1.   Describe the presidential election process from primaries to the general election.

2.   Explain the legislative action taken to try to reform campaign financing.

3.   Describe and explain the factors associated with voting.

4.   Discuss the Electoral College procedures and proposed reforms.

ANSWERS TO THE PRACTICE EXAM

Fill-in-the-blank.

1.   white, male
2.   recruited
3.   Political Consultant
4.   soft money
5.   tracking polls
6.   senators, representatives
7.   party-column
8.   reporting the news
9.   spin
10. corporate conglomerates

True/False.

1. F	3. F	5. T	7. T	9. T
2. T	4. T	6. F	8. T	10. T

Multiple Choice.

1. d	6. b	11. a	16. d
2. d	7. d	12. b	17. c
3. b	8. d	13. d	18. a
4. b	9. c	14. c	19. d
5. a	10. c	15. b	20. b

Short Essay Questions. Briefly address the major concepts raised by the following questions.

1. Explain the legislative action taken to try to reform campaign financing.
   - Congress in 1925 passed a series of acts called the Corrupt Practices Acts, which were largely ineffective.
   - The Hatch Act passed in 1939 put limits on the amount of money that political groups could contribute to political campaigns.
   - The Federal Election Campaign Act of 1972 replaced the past laws and instituted a major reform.
   - After the Watergate scandal, the Federal election Campaign Act of 1974 created more reform. It did the following:
     - Created the Federal Election Commission.
     - Provided public funding for presidential primaries and general elections.
     - Limited presidential campaign spending.
     - Limited contributions
     - Required disclosure.
   - 1976 Amendments to the law allowed for the creation of Political Action Committees.
   - Bipartisan Campaign Reform Act of 2002 prohibited soft money in federal elections.

2. Describe the presidential election process from primaries to the general election.
   - The presidential process is two different campaigns from January to November linked together by the political party's national conventions.
     - The presidential primary system begins with the Iowa caucus in January and New Hampshire primary in February. The winner of these elections is dubbed the front-runner by the media, which gives that candidate a big boost in their campaign.
     - States have moved their primary dates in recent years to try to have more influence in the nomination of presidential candidates. California has moved its primary to March, in a process that is known as front-loading. Southern states hold their primaries on the same date, known as Super Tuesday.
     - The caucuses and primaries select delegates, who go to the national convention. The main purpose of the national convention is to nominate the president and vice-president.
     - The president and vice-president begin the campaign to capture the office in the general election around Labor Day.

3. Discuss the Electoral College procedures and proposed reforms.
   - The Electoral College is the constitutionally required method for the selection of the president and vice-president.
   - Each state's electors are selected during the presidential election year. Each state has the number of electors equal to that state's number of senators (two) plus it number of representatives.
   - The slate of electors in a state is elected by the candidate, which has a plurality vote. In other words, the most votes of any candidate. It takes 270 electoral votes to win the presidency.

- The two major suggested reforms of the Electoral College are to elect the president by popular vote and require each elector by law to vote for the candidate that received the plurality.

4. Discuss the role of media and politics in presidential campaigns.
   - The functions of the media
     - The primacy of television
     - TV's influence on the political process
     - Media and political campaigns
     - Media importance

Chapter 10
THE CONGRESS

CHAPTER SUMMARY

Why was Congress Created?
The founders of the American Constitution believed that the bulk of government power should be in the hands of the legislative branch. The large and small state division at the constitutional convention created a bicameral Congress, with one house based on big-state population and the other based on small state equality in the senate. The differences between the institutions in this bicameral Congress were further emphasized with a two-year term for Representatives in the House and a six-year term for Senators.

The Functions of Congress
Congress has six basic functions, which include lawmaking, service to constituents, representation, oversight, public education, and conflict resolution. Lawmaking is the most obvious and important function of Congress. The idea for most legislation comes from outside, but Congress is solely responsible for approving legislation. Service to constituents is an important aspect of being reelected and is accomplished mostly by acting as an ombudsperson and doing casework. A member can represent their constituency by being a trustee, who uses their own judgment, an instructed delegate, who uses the constituents' judgment, or a politico, who uses both approaches depending on the issue. The oversight function is to make sure that the laws passed are enforced and administered the way in which they were intended. The public education function is an important part of helping to set the public agenda, which primarily occurs with the media. See Chapter 9. The final function is to resolve conflicts in society, which primarily arise because of scarce resources and differences in ideology.

The Powers of Congress
The first seventeen clauses of Article I, Section 8 of the constitution specify most of the enumerated powers of Congress. Beyond these specific powers is the "necessary and proper" clause, which has allowed for a greatly expanded national government power.

House-Senate Differences
Congress is composed of two very different but coequal chambers. The House is much larger at 435 members because it represents the population of the United States. The Senate is 100 members, which gives each of the fifty states two senators. See Table 10-1, which shows the major differences between the House and the Senate. The size difference of the two requires the House to have a Rules Committee to limit debate, while the Senate has unlimited debate, which sometimes leads to filibustering. The Senate, because of its smaller number and more powers from the Constitution, is considered the most prestigious of the institutions.

Congresspersons and the Citizenry: A Comparison
Members of Congress are more likely to be white, male, Protestant, and trained in higher-status occupations than the average citizen.

Congressional Elections
The process of electing members of Congress varies according to the election laws of each state from which they are elected. Many congressional candidates are self-recruited and have ties to the local district. In recent years, the costs of campaigns have really escalated. Two major issues have a major impact on congressional elections. These are the presidential election years, which can produce a "coattails" effect or a scandal, which can hurt the candidate, and the power of the incumbency, which makes it very difficult for a challenger to defeat the office holder. The office holder can use advertising of their name recognition, claim credit for government programs, or take positions on popular issues. In spite of the advantage of incumbency, in the 1994 election, voters swept the Democratic majority in both chambers of Congress out of power. This development with Democrat Bill Clinton in the presidency created a period of "divided government," which continued after the 2000 elections. In the 2002 elections, divided government ended as Republicans controlled the Presidency and both houses of Congress.

Congressional Apportionment

One of the most complicated aspects of congressional elections is the issue of reapportionment. Since representation in the House is based on population after the census every ten years, the seats of the House must be allocated according to the latest population figures. This is called reapportionment. The state legislatures will redistrict or redraw political boundaries to match the changes that have occurred in population. In the past, legislatures did not always carry out this constitutional responsibility. In the **Baker v. Carr** case (1962), the Supreme Court ruled that this issue could be reviewed by the court and that the legislatures had to use the principle of "one person, one vote" to redistrict. In **Reynolds v. Sims** (1964), the Court applied "one person, one vote" to both houses of the state legislature, and in **Wesberry v. Sanders** (1964), it was applied to Congress. One issue that has not been fully resolved by the courts is gerrymandering. This term refers to the manipulation of redistricting to give an advantage to one political party over the other one.

Pay, Perks, and Privileges

In 2004, members of Congress received salaries of $157,000 a year and receive a number of benefits, such as free parking, free medical care, generous pensions, liberal travel allowances, and free postage or franking privileges. They are able to hire an extensive professional staff and use the resources of the professional staff of many other government agencies. Members of Congress are also exempt from certain laws that apply to ordinary citizens.

The Committee Structure

The committees and sub-committees of Congress perform most of the actual work of creating legislation in Congress. Committees are commonly known as "little legislatures" because the committee is a microcosm of what happens in the legislature. There are five types of committees: standing, select, joint, conference, and the House Rules committee. Standing committees are the permanent committees that are given a specific area of legislative policy. Select committees are created for a limited time period and for a specific purpose. A joint committee is composed of members of both the House and Senate. A conference committee is a special joint committee created to achieve agreement on legislation. The House Rules committee is unique to the House and is necessary to set rules for the 435 members of the body. The leaders of House and Senate committees, called chairpersons, are selected by seniority among the members of the majority party in each chamber.

The Formal Leadership

The political parties organize the formal leadership of Congress. The leadership in the House is made up of the speaker, the majority and minority leaders, and party whips. The speaker of the House is the presiding officer of the House, a member of the majority party, and the most powerful member of the House. The majority leader is the leader of floor debate and cooperates with the speaker. The minority leader is the leader of the minority party and speaks for the President if the minor party controls the White House. Party officials called whips assist the leaders in Congress. The two most important formal leaders in the Senate are both ceremonial figures. The Constitution established the Vice-President as the presiding officer or President of the Senate. The Vice-President is rarely present for a meeting of the Senate. The Senate has elected a president pro tempore ("pro tem") to preside in the absence of the Vice-President. The real leadership power in the Senate is with the majority and minority floor leaders, who are assisted by whips.

How Members of Congress Decide

It is difficult to establish all of the factors that determine how a member of Congress will vote. The single best predictor of how a member will vote seems to be political party membership. Party membership can be influenced by cues from respected senior members and regional and ideological differences.

How a Bill Becomes Law

The process of how a bill becomes law begins with the bill being introduced to the House or Senate or both. A bill is referred to the appropriate committee and subcommittee, where the heart of the legislative process occurs. The content specialists in the committee then closely examine a bill. If the bill is voted favorably by the committee, it will be sent to the Rules committee in the House or scheduled for floor debate in the Senate. The bill will be debated and voted on by the entire House and Senate. If a bill has passed the House and Senate with a majority vote in slightly different form, it will be sent to a conference committee to work out the differences in the bill. If approved by both the House and Senate, the bill will be sent to the president for his signature or veto.

How Much Will the Government Spend?

The Constitution provides that all tax and spending bills must originate in the House of Representatives. Congress requires that the president prepares and submits the executive budget to Congress for their approval. Budget conflicts with the president led Congress to pass the Budget and Impoundment Control Act in 1974. The federal government operates on a fiscal-year budget cycle that begins on October 1 each year. The Office of Management and Budget reviews each agency's budget request and prepares a budget, which the president submits to Congress in January of each year. Congress then reviews the budget submitted by the president and decides on the first budget resolution in May, which establishes the overall budget spending. The second budget resolution is supposed to be passed October 1 with the budget for each government agency. Often, Congress does not pass the second budget resolution by October 1. Congress must then pass a temporary law, called a continuing resolution, to keep government agencies open until the new budget can be agreed upon.

The Congress: Why Is It Important Today?

To many voters, Congress spends too much time in political battles. One of the most important decisions that Congress makes is how much the government spends. When members of Congress go home to their districts, voters have the opportunity to argue for and against policy decisions.

KEY TERMS

Agenda setting — p. 340
Appropriations — p. 365
Authorization — p. 364
Bicameralism — p. 337
Casework — p. 340
Conference committee — p. 356
Conservative coalition — p. 361
Constituent — p. 337
Continuing resolution — p. 366
Direct primary — p. 347
Discharge petition — p. 354
Enumerated power — p. 341
Executive budget — p. 363
Fall review — p. 364
Filibustering — p. 343
First budget resolution — p. 366
Fiscal year (FY) — p. 364
Gerrymandering — p. 349
Instructed delegate — p. 339
Joint committee — p. 356
Justiciable question — p. 348
Lawmaking — p. 338

Logrolling — p. 338
Majority leader of the House — p.358
Minority leader of the House — p.358
Ombudsperson — p. 340
Oversight — p. 340
Reapportionment — p. 348
Redistricting — p. 348
Rules committee — p. 343
Safe seat — p. 357
Second budget resolution — p. 366
Select committee — p. 355
Senate majority leader — p. 359
Senate minority leader — p. 359
Seniority system — p. 356
Speaker of the House — p.357
Spring review — p.364
Standing committee — p. 355
Trustee — p. 339
Whip — p. 359

PRACTICE EXAM
(Answers appear at the end of this chapter.)

Fill-in-the-Blank. Supply the missing word(s) or term to complete the sentence.

1. The Founding Fathers believed that the bulk of the power that the national government would exercise should be in the hands of the _____.

2. According to the thinking of the Founding Fathers, the House was to be the _____ _____ chamber and the Senate was to be the chamber of the _____.

3. The division of a legislature into two separate assemblies is _____.

4. A legislator who is an agent of the voters who elected him or her and who votes according to the views of constituents is called a/an _____ _____ .

5. _____ is the process by which congress follows up on the laws it has enacted to ensure that they are being enforced and administered in the way Congress intended.

6. Under Senate Rule 22, debate may be ended by invoking _____ or shutting off discussion on a bill.

7. The impact that a strong presidential candidate has on the ballot is called _____.

8. In the 2004 election, _____ incumbent House candidates were reelected out of _____ running.

9. The process of electing members of Congress is controlled by _____ _____.

10. Committee chairs in congress are selected by _____.

True/False. Circle the appropriate letter to indicate if the statement is true or false.

T   F   1. The Founding Fathers believed that the bulk of the power of the national Government should be in the hands of the president.

T   F   2. The principle function of any legislature is lawmaking.

T   F   3. Instructed delegates mirror the views of the majority of the constituents whom elected them to power.

T   F   4. The Rules Committee is the most powerful committee in the Senate.

T   F   5. Members of Congress must be cautious about what they say on the floor of Congress because of the possibility of being sued for slander.

T   F   6. By far, the most important committees in Congress are the standing committees.

T   F   7. Party membership is the single best predictor of how a member of Congress will vote on issues.

T   F   8. If Congress does not approve a budget by the beginning of the fiscal year, the government can continue to operate on continuing resolutions.

T   F   9. All money bills must originate in the House of Representatives.

T   F   10. How much the government spends is one of the most serious issues for Congress today.

Multiple Choice. Circle the correct response.

1. The Senate is the chamber of the Congress that
    a. must first approve all money bills.
    b. must first approve amendments.
    c. ratifies treaties.
    d. has the first opportunity to override presidential vetoes.

2. The voting behavior of an instructed delegate would be to represent the
    a. majority view of his or her constituents.
    b. broad interests of society.
    c. interests of his or her party.
    d. president in voting in Congress.

3. Some functions are restricted to only one house of Congress. The Senate is the only house that can
    a. propose amendments.
    b. approve the budget.
    c. approve presidential appointments.
    d. investigate the president.

4. The <u>central</u> difference between the House and the Senate is that the
    a. House is much larger in membership than the Senate.
    b. House represents people, the Senate represents geography.
    c. Senate ratifies treaties.
    d. House first appropriates money.

5. Of the American population (2000 census), _____ percent are church members , yet _____ percent of Senators are church members.
    a. 61,100
    b. 100, 61
    c. 42,97
    d. 64, 35

6. For the House of representatives,
    a. each state is allowed two representatives.
    b. there is no set number of minimum or maximum for each state.
    c. each state is allowed at least one representative.
    d. membership for each state is determined by the House itself.

7. Most candidates for Congress must win the nomination for office in a
    a. party caucus.
    b. indirect primary.
    c. direct primary.
    d. party convention.

8. Midterm Congressional elections
    a. attract as many voters as presidential elections.
    b. attract more voters than presidential elections.
    c. usually result in the president's party losing seats in Congress.
    d. usually result in the president's party gaining seats in Congress.

9. The Supreme Court cases of Baker v. Carr, Reynolds v. Sims, and Wesberry v. Sanders all pertained to the issue of
    a. foreign policy.
    b. budget policy.
    c. reapportionment.
    d. campaign spending.

10. The principle of "one person, one vote" was first applied to congressional districts in the Supreme Court case of
    a. Baker v. Carr.
    b. Reynolds v. Sims.
    c. Wesberry v. Sanders.
    d. Plessy v. Ferguson.

11. Gerrymandering refers to the process of
    a. ending debate in the Senate.
    b. redrawing legislative boundaries.
    c. forcing a bill out of committee.
    d. selecting a committee chair.

12. The phrase "little legislatures" refers to the
    a. legislatures that exist in the states.
    b. committees in Congress.
    c. departments of the federal bureaucracy.
    d. interest groups that lobby Congress.

13. The "third house of Congress" refers to
    a. standing committees.
    b. select committees.
    c. special committees.
    d. conference committees.

14. In the House of Representatives, the majority leader
    a. acts as spokesperson for the majority party in the House.
    b. serves as Speaker of the House.
    c. is elected in a vote of all the members of the House.
    d. is rarely able to exert any meaningful leadership because of the dominance of the Speaker.

15. The congressional budget process was very disjointed until the passage of the
    a. Office of Management and Budget.
    b. Budget and Impoundment Control Act.
    c. Discharge Petition.
    d. Council of Economic Advisers.

16. The fiscal year (FY) of the federal government is
    a. January to December.
    b. April to February.
    c. October to September.
    d. July to June.

17. The federal agency that prepares the budget is the
    a. Economic Agency.
    b. Office of Management and Budget.
    c. Congress.
    d. Council of Economic Advisers.

18. A continuing resolution allows
    a. congresspersons to remain in office after their term.
    b. a nearly passed law to remain in the new session of Congress.
    c. government agencies to continue to function if a new budget is not passed.
    d. the President to set the budget without Congress.

19. The budget process of the federal government begins _____ before the start of the fiscal year.
    a. 1 to 1-1/2 years
    b. 2 years
    c. 6 months
    d. 3 months

20. One of the most important decisions for Congress that affects our lives every day is
    a. under representation of minority groups.
    b. how much the government spends.
    c. reforming the Electoral College.
    d. too many young people elected to Congress.

Short Essay Questions. Briefly address the major concepts raised by the following questions.

1. Explain the major functions of Congress.

2. Trace the development of congressional reapportionment.

3. Describe the leadership positions in the House of Representatives and the Senate.

4. Discuss the steps that a bill must take to become law.

ANSWERS TO THE PRACTICE EXAM

Fill-in-the-blank.

1. legislature
2. common people, elite
3. bicameralism
4. instructed delegate
5. oversight
6. cloture
7. "coattails"
8. 397, 404
9. state governments
10. seniority

True/False.

1.	F	3.	T	5.	F	7.	T	9.	T
2.	T	4.	F	6.	T	8.	T	10.	T

Multiple Choice.

1.	c	6.	c	11.	b	16.	c
2.	a	7.	c	12.	b	17.	b
3.	c	8.	c	13.	d	18.	c
4.	a	9.	c	14.	a	19.	a
5.	a	10.	c	15.	b	20.	b

Short Essay Questions. Briefly address the major concepts raised by the following questions.

1. Explain the major functions of Congress.
    - There are six major functions of Congress, which include lawmaking, service to constituents, representation, oversight, public education, and conflict resolution.
        - Lawmaking is the principal and most obvious function of a legislative body.
        - Service to constituents is primarily carried out by doing casework and by acting as an ombudsperson with government agencies.
        - Members of Congress can represent constituents by being a trustee or instructed delegate.
        - The oversight function is for Congress to follow up on laws enacted, to see that they are being enforced and administered as intended.
        - The public education function of Congress is to assist in agenda setting.
        - Conflict resolution is a key function for government to resolve issues of scarce resources and differences in societal goals.

2. Trace the development of congressional reapportionment.
    - The process of reapportionment is the allocation of seats in the House of Representatives to each state after each census.
    - The movement of people from rural areas to cities and suburbs created numerical malapportionment prior to 1960.

- In 1962, the Supreme Court in the case of **Baker v. Carr** ruled that the issue of reapportionment could be ruled on by the court on the basis of the "one person, one vote" principle.
- In 1964, the Supreme Court applied this principle to state legislatures in **Reynolds v. Sims** and to congressional districts in **Wesberry v. Sanders**.
- Gerrymandering and "minority-majority" are issues of reapportionment that remain unresolved.

3. Describe the leadership positions in the House of Representatives and the Senate.
   - Leadership in the House consists of the speaker, the majority and minority leaders, and party whips.
     - The Speaker is the most important leader in the House, who presides, makes appointments, schedules legislation, decides points of order, and refers bills.
     - The majority and minority leaders are elected in party caucus and act as spokespersons and leaders of their party.
     - Whips are assistants to the party leaders.
   - Leadership in the Senate consists of the vice-president, president pro tempore, majority and minority leaders, and party whips.
     - The Constitution creates the President of the Senate, the vice president, as the ceremonial leader of the Senate.
     - The Senate elects a ceremonial leader, president pro tempore, to preside over the Senate in the vice president's absence.
     - The real leadership power in the Senate rests with the majority and minority leaders.
     - Whips are assistants to Senate party leaders.

4. Discuss the steps that a bill must take to become law. See Figure 10-3 for an illustration of the entire legislative process.

   - The bill is introduced to the House or Senate or both.
   - The bill is referred to the appropriate committee.
   - The bill is referred to subcommittee.
   - The full committee reports out the bill.
   - The Rules Committee in the House establishes rules for the bill.
   - The entire House debates the bill and vote on it.
   - The same steps, except for the Rules Committee, occur in the Senate.
   - Conference action may be required to clear up differences between the House and Senate.
   - The bill goes to the president for approval or veto.

Chapter 11
THE PRESIDENT

CHAPTER SUMMARY

Who Can Become President?

The official requirements for becoming president are (1) a natural born citizen, (2) 35 years old, and (3) a fourteen year resident of the United States. The informal requirements suggest the president will be an older (54), white, Protestant male.

The Process of Becoming President

The voters do not directly vote for president and vice president, but instead vote for electors, who officially vote in the Electoral College. On a few occasions, the Electoral College has failed to elect a president, and the House of Representatives has had to make the decision. The Twelfth Amendment adopted in 1804 clarified one aspect of this process by separating the election of the president and vice president.

The Many Roles of the President

The Constitution has created five major roles or functions for the president. These are (1) chief of state, (2) chief executive, (3) commander in chief of the armed forces, (4) chief diplomat, and (5) chief legislator. The chief of state role is the ceremonial head of state role. See page 376 for a list of these activities. The chief executive role requires the president to "faithfully execute" the laws.

The federal bureaucracy assists the president to carry out his executive responsibilities, and the president has appointive power to fill some government office positions. Under his executive power, the president can grant reprieves and pardons for all federal crimes except in cases of impeachment. The president as commander in chief of the armed forces represents civilian control of the military. Presidents have probably exercised more authority in this role than any other. In 1973, Congress attempted to gain more control over military actions with the War Powers Resolution. In spite of this resolution, the powers of the president as commander in chief are still extensive. The role of chief diplomat gives the president the power to recognize foreign government, to make treaties with the approval of the Senate, and generally to conduct United States foreign policy. Presidents have greatly expanded their power in foreign policy through the use of executive agreements, which do not require Senate approval. The president's power as chief legislator consists of the annual State of the Union message and the power of the veto. The veto power was expanded to include a line-item veto power on spending bills, which was first used by President Clinton. The law creating the line-item veto was challenged in the case of **Clinton v. City of New York** and ruled unconstitutional in 1998 by the Supreme Court. Other presidential powers are given to the president by statute from Congress, express powers and inherent powers defined through practice.

The President as Party Chief and Superpolitician

Although the Constitution mentions nothing about political party leadership, the President is head of his political party. A major tool of the president as party leader is patronage. The president must be concerned about three different constituencies as he leads his party. These constituencies are the public in general, the members of the political parties, and the Washington community. How successful the president is with these constituencies is measured by his approval rating.

The Special Uses of Presidential Power

Presidents have four special powers and privileges. These are (1) emergency powers, (2) executive orders, (3) executive privilege, and until recently, (4) impoundment of funds. The power to act in a crisis or emergency powers of the president were first stated in the Supreme Court case of **United States v. Curtiss-Wright Export Corp** in 1936. Executive orders issued by the president, which must be published in the Federal Register, have the force of law. Executive privilege is the right of executive officials to withhold information from legislative committees on the basis of separation of powers. This concept was upheld in 1974 by the Supreme Court case of **United States v. Nixon**. Nixon had to turn over the Watergate tapes because executive privilege could not be used to hide evidence in a criminal case. The concept did not hold up under President Clinton's impeachment proceedings.

The Abuses of Executive Power and Impeachment

The constitution authorized the House to impeach and the Senate to remove the president, vice president, and other civil officials for "high Crimes and Misdemeanors." In the history of the United States, no president has been impeached and removed from office. President Andrew Johnson in 1868 was impeached and tried by the Senate, which failed to remove him by one vote. In 1974, the House Judiciary Committee recommended impeachment charges against President Nixon over the cover-up of the Watergate break-in. Nixon resigned the presidency before the full House voted impeachment charges. In 1998, the House Judiciary Committee recommended an impeachment inquiry against President Clinton over the cover-up of the Monica Lewinsky affair. The articles of impeachment were then sent to the Senate, which conducted a trial and acquitted President Clinton.

The Executive Organization

At the beginning of Franklin Roosevelt's tenure as president, the staff was 37. Today, the staff is over 600. The advisory group for the president, called the cabinet, began with four officials. Today, there are 14 officials, including 13 secretaries of various departments and the Attorney General. Modern presidents do not use the cabinet as an advisory group today but prefer to rely on informal advisers, called the kitchen cabinet. In 1939, President Franklin Roosevelt created by executive order the Executive Office of the President (EOP). The EOP consists of nine staff agencies that assist the president in carrying out all major duties. One of the most important agencies in the EOP is the White House Office, which includes most of the key personnel and advisers to the president. In recent presidencies, the chief of staff is in charge of coordinating the White House Office. The Council of Economic Advisers (CEA) was created in 1946 to advise the president on economic matters. President Nixon created the Office of Management and Budget (OMB) from the Bureau of the Budget in 1970. This agency prepares the federal budget, and advises the president on management techniques. The National Security Council brings together the foreign policy and military advisers to the president.

The Vice Presidency

The Constitution only gives the vice president the duty to preside over the Senate and vote in case of a tie vote. Traditionally vice presidents have been selected to balance the ticket and appeal to voters that the president does not appeal to. Eight times in our history the vice-president has become president because of the death of the president. Each time this has happened there was no provision to replace the vice president until the next election. In addition, there was no provision for a case of presidential incapacity. In 1967, the Twenty-fifth Amendment to the Constitution provided for both replacing the vice president and a process for presidential incapacity. The first use of the amendment occurred with the resignation of Nixon's vice president, Spiro Agnew. Congress confirmed Gerald Ford as the new vice president. When President Nixon resigned the next year, Gerald Ford became the first non-elected president in our history. President Ford selected with congressional approval Nelson Rockefeller to be vice president.

The Presidency: Why Is It Important Today?

The scope of the presidency has changed from chief clerk to world leader in the twentieth century. The president has become a "super star" with the help of media, and the image often obscures important policy issues. The task of regulating the economy and overseeing the government has become very difficult with the advent of "divided government." The role of the president in engaging the nation in military action is another important issue that will remain in the new century.

KEY TERMS

Advice and consent — p. 381
Appointment power — p. 377
Cabinet — p. 394
Chief diplomat — p. 381
Chief executive — p. 377
Chief legislator — p. 383

Chief of staff — p. 396
Commander in chief — p. 397
Constitutional power — p. 386
Diplomatic recognition — p. 381

Emergency power — p. 391
Executive agreement — p. 383
Executive Office of the President (EOP) — p. 395
Executive order — p. 391
Executive privilege — p. 392
Expressed power — p. 386
Federal register — p. 391
Head of state — p. 376
Impeachment — p. 393
Inherent power — p. 387
Kitchen cabinet — p. 394
Line-item veto — p. 386
National Security Council (NSC) — p. 396

Office of Management and Budget OMB) — p. 396
Pardon — p. 379
Patronage — p. 387
Pocket veto — p. 385
Reprieve — p. 379
State of the Union message — p.384
Statutory power — p. 386
Twelfth amendment — p. 376
Twenty-fifth Amendment — p. 399
Veto message — p. 384
War powers resolution — p. 380
White House Office — p. 396

PRACTICE EXAM
(Answers appear at the end of this chapter.)

Fill-in-the-Blank. Supply the missing word(s) or term to complete the sentence.

1. The _____ Amendment clarified aspects of Electoral College voting.

2. The president decorating war heroes is an example of his role as head _____ _____.

3. The president is constitutionally bound to enforce the acts of Congress, the judgments of federal courts, and treaties in his role as _____ _____.

4. The constitution gives the president the power to grant _____ and _____ for offenses against the United States except in cases of impeachment.

5. Presidential power in foreign affairs is greatly enhanced by the use of _____ _____ made between the president and other heads of state.

6. Powers given to the president by law are called _____ _____.

7. The formal indictment of the president for wrongdoing by the House of Representatives is called _____.

8. The presidential advisory group composed of the secretaries of the executive departments is called the _____.

9. The official responsible for coordinating the White House Office is the _____ _____ _____.

10. The only formal duty of the vice president found in the Constitution is to preside over the _____.

True/False. Circle the appropriate letter to indicate if the statement is true or false.

T   F   1. A presidential candidate cannot win the Electoral College vote without getting a majority of the popular vote.

T   F   2. In most democratic governments, the role of chief of state is given to someone other than the chief executive.

T   F   3. The president's extensive appointment powers allow him to control and run the federal bureaucracy to suit his desires.

T   F   4. The president may grant reprieves and pardons for all offenses against the United States except in cases of contempt of Court.

T   F   5. The president has the sole power to recognize or refuse to recognize foreign governments.

T   F   6. Executive agreements made by the president and the heads of other governments must be ratified by the Senate.

T   F   7. The presidential veto is an effective legislative tool because Congress rarely can override them.

T   F   8. Emergency powers are the most common example of inherent powers exercised by the president.

T   F   9. An executive order is the president's legislative power.

T   F   10. Most presidents have relied heavily on their cabinet members for advice in decision making.

Multiple Choice. Circle the correct response.

1. The most common occupation of presidents has been
   a. teachers.
   b. lawyers.
   c. businessmen.
   d. farmers.

2. In the event that no candidate receives a majority of the Electoral College votes, the president is selected by the
   a. Senate from the two candidates receiving the highest electoral votes.
   b. Senate from any candidates receiving electoral votes
   c. Congress from any person they choose to elect.
   d. House of Representatives choosing from the highest three candidates receiving electoral votes.

3. The activity most typical of the Chief of State role is
   a. developing military strategy.
   b. offering the State of the Union Address.
   c. negotiating treaties with foreign governments.
   d. receiving visiting chiefs of state at the White House.

4. The president can remove all of the following from office except
   a. federal judges.
   b. the heads of cabinet departments.
   c. individuals within the Executive Office of the President.
   d. political appointees.

5. The effect of the Constitutional requirement that the president "shall be the Commander in Chief of the Army and Navy," is to
   a. require the president to be a commissioned officer.
   b. distort the lines of authority within the command structure of the armed forces.
   c. require the president to take instruction at one of the service academies.
   d. place the armed forces under civilian, rather than military, control.

6. The role in which the president has probably exercised more authority than in any other role is
   a. Chief Administrator.
   b. Chief of his party.
   c. Commander-in-Chief.
   d. Chief Legislator.

7. The activity typical of the role of Chief Diplomat is
   a. vetoing foreign policy legislation.
   b. delivering the State of the Union Address.
   c. meeting with state governors to discuss federal aid.
   d. negotiating treaties with foreign governments.

8. A typical activity associated with the role of Chief Legislator is
   a. recognizing representatives from foreign governments.
   b. negotiating treaties with foreign governments.
   c. meeting with state party leaders to discuss campaign strategy.
   d. offering the annual State of the Union Address.

9. The only requirement of a president in issuing an executive order is that the executive order must
   a. pertain to legislatively authorized items.
   b. deal with only military matters.
   c. deal only with the Executive Office of the President.
   d. be published in the Federal Register.

10. Executive privilege
    a. means that no member of the executive branch can be prosecuted for any act while they are performing their job.
    b. is the concept that has been applied to the president's use of a pocket veto during a session of Congress.
    c. protects the president and his cabinet from impeachment proceedings.
    d. involves the ability of the president to withhold certain information from congress and/or the courts.

11. The last president impeached by the House of Representatives was
    a. Lyndon Johnson.
    b. Andrew Johnson.
    c. Richard Nixon.
    d. Bill Clinton.

12. The agency that includes most of the key personal and political advisers to the president is in the
    a. Cabinet.
    b. Congress.
    c. White House Office.
    d. National Security Council.

13. Which statement is correct concerning the vice president's job?
    a. The Constitution gives several important powers to the vice president.
    b. The Constitution makes the vice president the number one advisor to the president.
    c. Earlier vice president had more to do than our recent vice president did.
    d. The constitution does not give much power to the vice president.

14. The Constitutional amendment establishing procedures for presidential succession and disability is the
    a. Twelfth Amendment.
    b. Twenty-Fourth Amendment.
    c. Twenty-Fifth Amendment.
    d. Twenty-Seventh Amendment.

15. The question of who shall be president if both the president and vice president die is answered by the
    a. Twenty-Fifth Amendment.
    b. special election to fill the vacancy.
    c. Succession Act of 1947.
    d. Twelfth Amendment.

16. The only President to use the line-item veto was
    a. Reagan.
    b. George H. Bush.
    c. Clinton.
    d. Nixon.

17. The constituency that measures the presidential performance on a daily basis is the
    a. party constituency.
    b. Congress.
    c. Washington community.
    d. media in rural areas.

18. Which office is third in the line of succession to the presidency?
    a. Speaker of the House
    b. Secretary of State
    c. Senate president pro tempore
    d. Attorney General

19. The emergency powers of the president were confirmed in
    a. U.S. v. Curtiss-Wright Export Corp.
    b. Youngstown Steel and Tube Co. v. Sawyer.
    c. U.S. v. Nixon.
    d. Train v. City of New York.

20. Which of the following is not in the Executive Office of the President (EOP)?
    a. White House Office Staff
    b. Office of the Vice President
    c. Council of Economic Advisers
    d. Office of Management and Budget

Short Essay Questions. Briefly address the major concepts raised by the following questions.

1. Identify and explain the roles of the president.

2. Trace the development of the sources of presidential power.

3. Describe the organization of the executive branch and how it has evolved over time.

4. Discuss the evolving role for the vice president as an advisor and successor to the president.

ANSWERS TO THE PRACTICE EXAM

Fill-in-the-blank.

1. Twelfth
2. of, state
3. chief executive
4. reprieve, pardon
5. executive, agreements
6. statutory, power
7. impeachment
8. cabinet
9. chief, of, staff
10. senate

True/False.

1. F	3. F	5. T	7. T	9. T
2. T	4. F	6. F	8. T	10. F

Multiple Choice.

1. b	6. c	11. d	16. c
2. d	7. d	12. c	17. c
3. d	8. d	13. d	18. c
4. a	9. d	14. c	19. a
5. d	10. d	15. c	20. b

Short Essay Questions. Briefly address the major concepts raised by the following questions.

1. Identify and explain the roles of the president.
   - There are five constitutional roles of the president. These are (1) chief of state, (2) chief executive, (3) commander in chief, (4) chief diplomat, and (5) chief legislator.
   - The chief of state role consists of ceremonial functions, such as decorating war heroes, hosting chiefs of state, telephoning sports and space heroes, and dedicating parks.
   - The chief executive role is to see that the laws are carried out. The president makes appointments of key individuals to carry out this function. He can also grant a reprieve and a pardon under executive authority.
   - Commander in chief is the concept of civilian control of the military. This is probably the president's most powerful role.
   - The chief diplomat role involves the making of treaties with the consent of the Senate and recognizing foreign governments as legitimate.
   - The chief legislator role includes the State of the Union message every year and the use of veto power in relationship to laws passed by Congress.

2. Discuss the special uses of presidential power.
   - Include a discussion of emergency powers.
   - Executive orders.
   - Executive privilege.
   - Impoundment of funds.

3. Describe the organization of the executive branch and how it has evolved over time.
   - The administration of George Washington developed an advisory group, the cabinet, composed of the heads of the executive departments.
   - Beginning with President Andrew Jackson, presidents used an informal group of advisors called the kitchen cabinet.
   - President Franklin Roosevelt greatly expanded the administrative staff of the president by the creation of the Executive Office of the President (EOP) in 1939. The key parts of the EOP are:
     - White House Office, which is coordinated by the chief of staff and provides the president with what ever he needs to carry out his duties.
     - Council of Economic Advisers (CEA) advises the president on economic policy.
     - The Office of Management and Budget (OMB) prepares the budget and advises the president on management and planning.
     - The National Security Council advises the president on military and security issues.

4. Discuss the evolving role for the vice president as an advisor and successor to the president.
   - The only role for the vice president mentioned in the Constitution is to preside over the Senate.
   - Vice Presidents have traditionally been selected to balance the ticket.
   - Eight vice presidents have become presidents because of the death of the president.
   - The Constitution provided no process to select a new vice president.
   - The Twenty-fifth Amendment provides for a process to select a new vice president and for a case of presidential disability.
   - The Succession Act of 1947 provides for the situation in which both the president and vice president die.

Chapter 12
THE BUREAUCRACY

CHAPTER SUMMARY

The Nature of Bureaucracy

Bureaucracy is defined as a large organization that is structured hierarchically to carry out specific functions. Bureaucracy can exist in both the public and private sectors. Public bureaucracies do not have a single set of leaders, are not organized to make a profit, are supposed to maximize costs, and are not necessarily efficient or responsive to change. The lack of government control of industry in the U.S. does not mean that administrative agencies do not regulate private industry. There are several different theories about how bureaucracies function. The Weberian model viewed bureaucracies as rational, hierarchical organizations in which power flows from the top down. The Acquisitive model focused on the belief that top-level bureaucrats always try to expand their budget and staff. The Monopolistic model believed that bureaucracies are like monopolies in that they are less efficient and more costly to operate. The federal bureaucracy in the U.S. enjoys a greater degree of autonomy than in other countries because of its size, federal system, and lack of ownership of enterprises.

The Size of the Bureaucracy

The federal bureaucracy began with three departments, State, War, and Treasury, and the office of Attorney General in 1789, consisting of a handful of employees. Today, the fourteen executive departments of government and other agencies employ approximately 2.7 million employees.

The Organization of the Federal Bureaucracy

The federal bureaucracy has four major types of structures. These are (1) cabinet departments, (2) independent executive agencies, (3) independent regulatory agencies, and (4) government corporations. The fourteen cabinet departments, described as line organizations, are the major part of the federal bureaucracy. Independent executive agencies are bureaucratic organizations that are not part of an executive department, but still report directly to the president. Independent regulatory agencies are responsible for regulating a particular sector of the economy in the public interest. The first agency established was the Interstate Commerce Commission (ICC) in 1887. Government corporations are agencies that administer a quasi-business enterprise. The U.S. Postal Service is a good example of this type of bureaucratic structure.

Staffing the Bureaucracy

There are two categories of bureaucrat, political appointees and civil servants. Political appointees are selected to the top positions in the government by the president. The average term of a political appointee is two years. The career civil servants, who make up the bulk of the bureaucracy, can afford to wait out political appointees that they do not agree with. The federal civil service began in 1789 with a so-called natural aristocracy of society's "best citizens." When Andrew Jackson became President, he implemented the spoils system by awarding government jobs to his political supporters and friends. In 1883, replacing it with a merit system reformed the spoils system, and the Civil Service Reform Act or Pendleton Act was passed. This act created the Civil Service Commission to administer the personnel service. In 1939, the Hatch Act was passed to protect government workers from political manipulation. Finally, the Civil Service Reform Act of 1978 created the Office of Personnel Management (OPM) and the Merit Systems Protection Board (MSPB).

Modern Attempts at Bureaucratic Reform

The government continues to attempt reforms of the bureaucracy and to make it more responsive to the needs of U.S. citizens. In 1976, congress passed the Government in the Sunshine Act. This law required all multi-headed federal agencies to conduct their business regularly in public session. Sunset legislation is designed to remove agencies on a regular basis, unless they are recreated with legislative action. Congress has never adopted this law, but most state legislatures have this law. Another approach to bureaucratic reform is to contract out services from the private sector to produce more efficient service. The Government Performance and Results Act of 1997 was designed to improve efficiency in the federal work force. Agencies were to set goals and establish a means of measuring if the goals were reached. The Merit Systems Protection Board (MSPB) created in 1978 was designed in part to protect whistleblowers, who would report bureaucratic waste and inappropriate behavior.

Bureaucrats as Politicians and Policymakers

Congress is unable to oversee the day-to-day administration of its programs. Congress delegates this authority to administrative agencies through what is called enabling legislation. Rulemaking by these agencies does not take place in vacuum, but occurs in the public arena because new regulations must be published in the Federal Register. Groups falling under regulation can engage in a process called negotiated ruling making. This process allowed individuals and groups to participate in the final rulemaking. Theories of bureaucracy once assumed that bureaucrats do not make policy decisions but merely enforce these decisions. The concepts of iron triangle and issue networks hold that bureaucrats do play a major role in policy decisions.

Congressional Control of the Bureaucracy

Although Congress cannot oversee the day-to-day operations of the bureaucracy, it can still control the bureaucracy by authorization and appropriation of funds and by investigation and oversight hearings.

The Bureaucracy: Why Is It Important Today?

Attempts to reform bureaucracy will continue in this century. Competition in the private marketplace will continue to influence government bureaucracy. The actual job of the federal bureaucracy will never disappear as long as government exists, and reforms will be needed on a continual basis to make the bureaucracy accountable to the citizens.

KEY TERMS

Acquisitive model — p. 408
Administrative agency — p. 409
Bureaucracy — p. 407
Cabinet department — p. 412
Capture — p. 416
Civil Service Commission — p. 420
Enabling legislation — p. 425
Government corporation — p. 417
Government in the Sunshine Act — p. 421
Independent executive agency — p. 415
Independent regulatory agency — p. 415

Iron triangle — p. 427
Issue network — p. 428
Merit system — p. 420
Monopolistic model — p. 408
Pendleton Act — p. 420
Privatization — p. 423
Spoils system — p. 419
Sunset legislation — p. 422
Weberian model — p. 408
Whistleblower — p. 424

PRACTICE EXAM
(Answers appear at the end of this chapter.)

Fill-in-the-Blank. Supply the missing word(s) or term to complete the sentence.

1. A _____ is the name given to a large organization that is structured hierarchically and is supposed to carry out specific functions.

2. The classic model of the modern bureaucracy is the _____ model.

3. The major service organizations of the federal government are the fourteen _____ _____.

4. _____ _____ _____ are bureaucratic organizations that are not located within a department and report directly to the president.

5. The earliest independent regulatory agency to be created was the _____ _____ _____.

6. The form of bureaucratic organization borrowed from business is the _____ _____.

7. The president generally associated with the spoils system is _____ _____.

8. Replacing government services with services from the private sector is called _____.

9. The three-way alliance among legislators, bureaucrats, and interest groups to benefit their respective interests is called the _____ _____.

10. The law that specifics the name, purpose, functions, and powers of an agency is _____ _____.

True/False. Circle the appropriate letter to indicate if the statement is true or false.

T   F   1.   Modern presidents have been able to exert power over the bureaucracy in order to shape it to their own desires.

T   F   2.   The federal bureaucracy in the United States is much more controlled and restricted than is true in other countries.

T   F   3.   Cabinet departments can be described in management terms as line organizations.

T   F   4.   Regulatory agencies are independent because they are administered independently of all three branches of government.

T   F   5.   The assassination of President James Garfield had an impact on Civil Service Reform.

T   F   6.   The Hatch Act prohibits federal civil service employees from engaging in political campaigns.

T   F   7.   Today, few states have sunset laws.

T   F   8.   Privatization of government services is a reform that has been most successful at the local level of government.

T   F   9.   Today, agencies and departments of government do not play an important role in policymaking because of tight control by Congress.

T   F   10.   Congress can call on the General Accounting Office to investigate bureaucratic agencies.

Multiple Choice. Circle the correct response.

1. A basic distinction between private corporations and public bureaucracies is that private corporations
   a. have managers and public bureaucracies do not.
   b. are organized to make a profit and public bureaucracies are not.
   c. are efficient and public bureaucracies are not.
   d. are generally large, complex enterprises, and Congress keeps public bureaucracies small.

2. The view that top-level bureaucrats will always try to expand the size of budgets is the theory of the
   a. Weberian Model.
   b. Acquisitive Model.
   c. Monopolistic Model.
   d. Garage Can Model.

3. The image of the bureaucracy as a noncompetitive organization is offered by the
   a. Garbage Can Model.
   b. Acquisitive Model.
   c. Monopolistic Model.
   d. Weberian Model.

4. Since 1970, most of the growth in government employment has occurred at the
    a. municipal level.
    b. state and local level.
    c. national level.
    d. county level.

5. The two groups of people in government who may call themselves bureaucrats are
    a. members of Congress and their appointees.
    b. the president and cabinet.
    c. political appointees and civil servants.
    d. state employees and members of Congress.

6. Thomas Jefferson brought into public service the so-called "natural aristocracy," which refers to
    a. a cadre of permanent civil servants.
    b. permanent patronage appointments.
    c. a small ruling clique whose membership is based on birth, wealth, and ability.
    d. loyal servants.

7. The Civil service Reform Act (Pendleton Act) had the effect of
    a. establishing in law the spoils system for political appointment.
    b. establishing the principle of employment on the basis of open competitive exams.
    c. preventing the best qualified people from being employed by the government.
    d. allowing corruption and graft to enter the employment practices of government.

8. The idea of sunset legislation was first suggested by President
    a. Franklin Roosevelt.
    b. Jimmy Carter.
    c. Abraham Lincoln.
    d. Ronald Reagan.

9. The major require imposed by the "Government in the Sunshine Act" is that
    a. federal agencies and commissions can have open meetings.
    b. information and individuals and companies can be made public.
    c. secret meetings may take place within the government.
    d. all multi-headed federal agencies conduct their business regularly in public session.

10. Sunset legislation refers to
    a. the idea that Congress must reauthorize programs annually.
    b. legislation that protects a program so that the sun will never set on the program.
    c. the idea of automatic program termination after a prescribed period unless Congress reauthorizes it.
    d. built-in protections for program continuation.

11. Congress created agencies within the federal bureaucracy to
    a. review proposed legislation.
    b. implement legislation passed by Congress.
    c. act as a sounding board for new laws.
    d. control the actions of the president.

12. The "iron triangle" refers to
    a. a policy of controlling information through censorship.
    b. the alliance of mutual benefit formed between an agency, its client group, and congressional committees.
    c. the mathematical formula used by the bureaucracy to determine benefit payments.
    d. an alliance between Congress, the president, and big business to control the economy.

13. The ultimate check that Congress has over the bureaucracy is the ability to
    a. hire and fire members of boards and commissions.
    b. write legislation in specific terms so that the bureaucracy will not be able to interpret the meaning of laws.
    c. withhold the appropriations of money to the bureaucracy.
    d. influence the president to take action against a bureaucrat.

14. Negotiated rulemaking involves federal agencies in negotiations with
    a. Congress.
    b. the president.
    c. the courts.
    d. parties to be affected by a new rule.

15. Issue networks are
    a. another name for "iron triangles."
    b. a more complex concept than "iron triangles" that illustrates how experts support issues on a particular policy position.
    c. an attempt by the media to manipulate public opinion on a particular issue.
    d. insider relationships within Congress to protect congressional benefits.

16. An administrative unit directly accountable to the president is called a(n)
    a. Executive Office of the President (EOP).
    b. merit system.
    c. line organization.
    d. Bureau of the President (BOP).

17. The Hatch Act provided for
    a. testing workers to determine who should be hired.
    b. prohibiting civil service workers from active political campaigning.
    c. protection for whistleblowers.
    d. privatization of government positions.

18. Since Congress is unable to oversee the day-to-day administration of programs, it has
    a. created whistleblower legislation.
    b. created enabling legislation.
    c. created the Federal Register.
    d. created "issue networks."

19. Negotiated rulemaking begins when an agency publishes the subject and scope of a new rule in the
    a. broadcast media.
    b. "issue networks."
    c. Federal Register.
    d. appropriate committee of Congress.

20. Which of the following do not conduct investigations for Congress?
    a. congressional committees
    b. the Federal Register
    c. the General Accounting Office
    d. the Congressional Budget Office

Short Essay Questions. Briefly address the major concepts raised by the following questions.

1.   Identify and explain several theories of bureaucracy.

2.   Discuss the different types of government agencies and organizations in the federal bureaucracy.

3.   Describe the recent reforms in the federal civil service.

4.   Explain the iron triangle and issue network models of the bureaucracy.

ANSWERS TO THE PRACTICE EXAM

Fill-in-the-blank.

1.   bureaucracy
2.   Weberian
3.   cabinet departments
4.   Independent executive agencies
5.   Interstate Commerce Commission
6.   government corporation
7.   Andrew Jackson
8.   privatization
9.   iron triangle
10. enabling legislation

True/False.

1. F	3. T	5. T	7. F	9. F
2. F	4. T	6. T	8. T	10. T

Multiple Choice.

1. b	6. c	11. b	16. c
2. b	7. b	12. b	17. b
3. c	8. a	13. c	18. b
4. b	9. d	14. d	19. c
5. c	10. c	15. b	20. b

Short Essay Questions.

1.   Identify and explain several theories of bureaucracy.
   *   There are three basic theories: (1) The Weberian model, (2) The Acquisitive model, and (3) The Monopolistic model.
       *   The classic or Weberian model viewed bureaucracy as rational, hierarchical organization in which power flows from the top downward and decisions are based on logic and data.
       *   The Acquisitive model focused on the concept that top level bureaucrats will want to maximize the size of their budgets and staff. The bureaucrat will try to "sell" their public service to Congress and the public.
       *   The Monopolistic model emphasized that bureaucracies are like monopolistic business firms because they have no competition. Monopolies tend to be less efficient and more costly to operate. This model arguing for the privatizing of some bureaucratic functions.

2. Discuss the different types of government agencies and organizations in the federal bureaucracy.
   - There are four major types of bureaucratic structures. They are (1) cabinet departments, (2) independent executive agencies, (3) independent regulatory agencies, and (4) government corporations.
     - Cabinet departments are the fourteen executive departments, headed by a secretary, except for the Justice Department headed by the Attorney General. These are the major service organizations of the national government.
     - Independent executive agencies are federal agencies not part of a cabinet department but report directly to the president. A good example of this kind of agency is the Central Intelligence Agency (CIA).
     - Independent regulatory agencies are agencies administered independently of all three branches of government because they perform the functions of all three branches. A good example is the Federal Communication Commission (FCC), which regulates all communication by telegraph, cable, telephone, radio, and television.
     - Government corporations are government agencies that administer a quasi-business enterprise. A good example is the U.S. Postal Service, which at one time was a cabinet department.

3. Describe the recent reforms in the federal civil service.
   - The important actual and proposed recent reforms include sunshine laws, sunset laws, contracting out, efficiency incentives, and more protection for whistleblowers.
     - Government in the Sunshine Act required all multi-headed federal agencies to hold public meetings.
     - Sunset laws require agencies to be terminated automatically at the end of a designated period, unless specifically reauthorized. This law has never been implemented by Congress, but most states have passed sunset laws.
     - Contracting out government services to private sector providers has been most successful at the local level for services like trash collection.
     - The Government Performance and Results Act of 1997 was designed to get government agencies to set goals and create a measurement system to document if goals were reached.
     - In spite of the Whistle-Blower Protection Act of 1989, individuals who bring to public attention gross government inefficiency or illegal action are not protected from losing their job.

4. Explain the iron triangle and issue network models of the bureaucracy.
   - The iron triangle is a way of describing the bureaucracy's role in the policy making process.
     - It consists of a three-way alliance among legislators in Congress, bureaucrats, and interest groups in a given policy area. Some examples are agricultural policy, weapon systems policy, and crime policy.
   - Issue networks is a more complex way to describe the bureaucracy's role in the policy making process.
     - An issue network consists of individuals or groups of experts that support a particular policy position on a given issue. This includes scholars, media, and others not usually considered part of the iron triangle theory.

Chapter 13
THE COURTS

CHAPTER SUMMARY

The Common Law Tradition

The concept of common law originated in England as judge-made law, a body of law that grew out of judicial decisions shaped by prevailing custom. This concept has influenced the American judicial system. The two main components of common law are precedent, which is a court ruling that will bear on subsequent legal decisions in similar cases, and *stare decisis*, which means to stand on decided cases.

Sources of American Law

The major sources of American law are federal and state constitutions, statutes passed by legislative bodies, administrative law, and case law. Constitutions set forth the general organization, powers, and limits of government. The U.S. Constitution is the supreme law of the land. Statutes or ordinances passed by national, state, and local governments have increasingly become important as courts apply these concepts to the general framework of common law. Case law is the rules and principles announced in court decisions, usually appeals courts.

The Federal Court System

The United States has a dual court system made up of the federal court structure and the courts of the fifty states. The federal courts are the U.S. district courts, which are the trial courts, thirteen U.S. courts of appeals, and the U.S. Supreme Court. The only court created in the U.S. Constitution is the Supreme Court, and it is the supreme law of the land. The state courts created by state constitutions are also under the authority of the U.S. Supreme Court. There is a common process that is followed by both court systems. The two parties in a lawsuit are the plaintiff, who initiates the suit, and the defendant, against whom the suit is brought. In recent years, interest groups have become more important in lawsuits because they litigate, that is, bring the case to trial. Interest groups can also influence the judicial process by *amicus curiae* briefs, which express a group's viewpoint on the case. Class-action suits are also brought by groups to benefit all citizens who are affected by the same situation.

The Supreme Court at Work

The Supreme Court term is from October to June each year. The Court is not required to hear a particular case, but several factors affect its decision. These factors include a legal question on which separate lower courts have ruled differently and pressure from the solicitor general of the U.S. to review a case. The solicitor general represents the government in cases before the Supreme Court and is sometimes referred to as the "Tenth Justice." The Court will issue a *writ of certiorari* if it decides to hear a case. It takes four justices to agree to hear a case. This is called the rule of four. The Court decides a case by a process that begins with oral arguments by the attorneys representing the two parties. The justices will meet in private conference to discuss the arguments and decide the case. The decision can be unanimous, which happens rarely, a majority decision, a concurring opinion, in which a justice wishes to emphasize a particular part of the decision, or a dissenting opinion, which is important because it can form the basis for the creation of a new majority or precedent in the future.

The Selection of Federal Judges

All federal judges are appointed by the president with the advice and consent of the Senate for a life-time term. The concept of senatorial courtesy allows a senator of the president's political party to exercise control over the federal judge vacancies in his or her state, particularly for the district court positions. Senatorial courtesy does not apply to Court of Appeals and Supreme Court appointments. The Supreme Court appointments are among the most important appointments that the president makes. Ideology plays a major role in the selection process for federal judges. Most presidents select judges of their own political party and ideology for the federal courts. Clinton has selected more women and members of minority groups to federal judgeships than any president before him. Ideology can also influence the Senate confirmation process.

Policymaking and the Courts

The battles over judicial appointments reflect the growing importance of the judiciary in policymaking through the tool of judicial review. Judicial review was established by the Supreme Court's decision in *Marbury v. Madison* (1803). Judges hold different views of the Court's role in policymaking. Judicial activism is a doctrine holding that the Supreme Court should take an active role in using its powers to check the other institutions of government when they exceed their authority. Judicial restraint rests on the principle that the Court should defer to the decisions made by the institutions elected by the people. The current court named for Chief Justice William Rehnquist, is a more conservative court than in the past. President Clinton's appointments to the court have brought about a more balanced court between liberal and conservative. See textbook for the current court members and ideological breakdown on page 453. The extensive influence of the Court today has produced a public debate about the amount of power the court has. Some critics want to see the power of the Court reduced.

What Checks Our Courts?

The executive, the legislature, the public, and the judiciary itself check the power of the courts. The executive branch carries out judicial rulings; the court does not have enforcement powers. The president also exercises control over the federal courts by his appointment of new judges. Congress must authorize funding to implement court decisions and can pass new laws in response to court decisions or begin the constitutional amendment process. Public opinion can limit the power of the court since it has no enforcement powers; its authority is linked to its stature in the eyes of the public. Finally, the traditions of the court, including its refusal to hear political questions, which the court believe should be decided by the elected branches. All these factors offer protection to the public from excessive court power.

The Judiciary: Why Is It Important Today?

The judiciary through judicial review provides a check on the power of Congress and the president. The Court has interpreted the constitution to provide for concepts such as the right to privacy. The judiciary is also important for providing stability to our society by allowing controversial issues to be decided in a peaceful way.

KEY TERMS

Affirm — p. 446
amicus curiae brief — p. 443
appellate court — p. 438
broad construction — p. 452
case law — p. 437
class-action suit — p. 443
common law — p. 435
concurring opinion — p. 446
dissenting opinion — p. 446
diversity of citizenship — p. 437
federal question — p. 437
general jurisdiction — p. 4438
judicial activism — p. 451
judicial implementation — p. 455
judicial restraint — p. 468
jurisdiction — p. 437
limited jurisdiction — p. 348
litigate — p. 441

majority opinion — p. 446
opinion — p. 445
oral arguments — p. 445
political questions — p. 457
precedent — p. 435
remand — p. 446
reverse — p. 446
rule of four — p. 445
senatorial courtesy — p. 447
stare decisis — p. 435
strict construction — p. 452
trail court — p. 438
unanimous opinion — p. 446
writ of certiorari — p. 445

PRACTICE EXAM
(Answers appear at the end of this chapter.)

Fill-in-the-Blank. Supply the missing word(s) or term(s) to complete the sentence.

1. The body of judge-made law that developed from England and is still used today in the United States is called _____ _____.

2. The practice of deciding new cases with reference to former decisions is based upon the doctrine of _____ _____.

3. The United States' dual court system consists of both _____ courts and _____ courts.

4. The Supreme Court's decision to hear a case is determined by the rule _____ _____.

5. A _____ _____ suit filed by an individual seeks damages for "all persons similarly situated."

6. By _____ of _____ the Supreme Court orders a lower court to send it the record of a case for review.

7. A _____ opinion is an opinion written by a Supreme Court justice who agrees with the majority opinion but for different reasons.

8. About 20% of Supreme Court appointments are _____ by the Senate.

9. Court decisions are translated into action by _____ _____.

10. Justices advocating the doctrine of _____ _____ believe the Supreme Court should defer to decisions made by elected representatives.

True/False. Circle the appropriate letter to indicate if the statement is true or false.

T   F   1. Most of American law is based on the English legal system.

T   F   2. Case law includes judicial interpretations of common law.

T   F   3. Federal court jurisdiction is less limited than state court jurisdiction because the federal government has jurisdiction over all the country.

T   F   4. Federal courts have authority to rule on all issues relating to state laws and federal matters.

T   F   5. Interest groups no longer use *amicus curiae* briefs to influence Supreme Court decisions.

T   F   6. Federal judges are either appointed or elected depending upon the type of court.

T   F   7. The nomination of Supreme Court justices belongs solely to the president.

T   F   8. Ideology no longer plays a very important role in a president's choice for the Supreme Court.

T   F   9. The makeup of the federal judiciary is typical of the American public.

T   F   10. The ideology of the Rehnquist court is more conservative with respect to states' rights.

Multiple-Choice. Circle the correct response.

1. *Stare decisis* is a doctrine
    a.   enabling court decisions to vary from case to case.
    b.   providing guidance to judges when common law does not apply.
    c.   encouraging the following of precedent or previous court decisions.
    d.   requiring hearings about complaints arising from regulations.

2. The level of trial courts in the federal judicial hierarchy is the
    a.   District courts.
    b.   Court of Appeals.
    c.   Supreme court.
    d.   state courts.

3. Appellate jurisdiction means the authority of a court to
    a.   serve as a trial court.
    b.   hear cases for the first time.
    c.   review decisions from a lower court.
    d.   establish grand juries.

4. A *writ of certiorari* is defined as an order
    a.   compelling an official to carry out his responsibilities.
    b.   guaranteeing the right to a fair and impartial trial by jury.
    c.   preventing some action from being carried out.
    d.   to a lower court to send a case to the higher court for review.

5. A *writ of certiorari* is issued by the Supreme Court only when
    a.   a majority of justices vote for such a request.
    b.   four justices vote for such a request.
    c.   a unanimous Court supports such a request.
    d.   the Solicitor General approves such a request.

6. The official who represents the national government in the Supreme Court is the
    a.   Attorney General.
    b.   Solicitor General.
    c.   Vice-President.
    d.   Chief Justice.

7. A Justice who accepts the majority decision but not the reasons for it may write his/her own
    a.   minority opinion.
    b.   majority opinion.
    c.   *amicus curiae* opinion.
    d.   concurring opinion.

8. In terms of enforcement powers, the Supreme Court
    a.   has now acquired its own police force.
    b.   relies upon the good will of the public to see that its decisions are enforced.
    c.   must rely on other units of government to carry out its decisions.
    d.   does not make decisions that have to be enforced.

9. Dissenting opinions in a Supreme Court decision are important because
    a.   they allow justices to make symbolic statements.
    b.   they agree with the majority opinion, but for different reasons.
    c.   they often form the basis for arguments that reverse decisions and establish new precedent.
    d.   they allow opposition groups to express their opinions before the court.

10. Senatorial courtesy is a concept that
    a. allows the president to pick his choice for judge.
    b. can veto a president's choice for judge.
    c. applies only to Supreme Court nominations.
    d. applies only to state court nominations.

11. The courts that have become "stepping-stones" to appointment to the Supreme Court are the
    a. District Courts.
    b. State Supreme Courts.
    c. Courts of Appeals.
    d. Tax Court.

12. In terms of judicial philosophy, Chief Justice William Rehnquist is know as a
    a. liberal justice.
    b. swing vote.
    c. conservative justice.
    d. moderate pragmatist.

13. The justices who believe that the Court should use its power to alter or challenge the policy direction of Congress, state legislatures, or administrative agencies are advocating
    a. judicial restraint.
    b. judicial activism.
    c. strict constructionism.
    d. moderate pragmatism.

14. The tradition of the Court has led justices to refuse to hear cases which are
    a. justiciable disputes.
    b. political questions.
    c. between citizens of different states.
    d. a real controversy.

15. The appointments of President Clinton to the Supreme Court have elevated the number of
    a. women to record numbers.
    b. Democrats to record numbers.
    c. minority members to record numbers.
    d. liberal members to record numbers.

16. Case law refers to
    a. a case involving federal law.
    b. a case heard by the Supreme Court.
    c. rules and principles announced in court decisions.
    d. a justiciable dispute.

17. The concept of judicial review was established in the case of
    a. Marbury v. Madison.
    b. McCulloch v. Maryland.
    c. Common law.
    d. Brown v. Board of Education of Topeka.

18. In several 2000 cases, the Supreme Court ruled that _____ had overreached authority under the commerce clause.
    a. the President
    b. Congress
    c. State governments
    d. Federal bureaucracy

19. A justiciable dispute or controversy is
    a. the same as a political questions.
    b. the same as *stare decisis.*
    c. disputes that arise out of actual cases.
    d. a case decided by the Supreme Court.

20. The U.S. Supreme Court overturning the Florida Supreme Court over vote counting in the 2000 Presidential election, surprised many observers because
    a. of judicial review.
    b. of support of Civil Rights cases.
    c. of support of rights of Accused cases.
    d. of support of state rights cases.

Short Essay Questions. Briefly address the major concepts raised by the following questions.

1. Identify and explain the common law tradition and other major sources of American law.

2. Discuss the process the Supreme Court uses to decide cases.

3. Describe the presidential appointment process for federal judges.

4. Explain the checks or limitations on the power of the federal courts.

ANSWERS TO THE PRACTICE EXAM

Fill-in-the-Blank.

1. common law
2. *stare decisis*
3. state, federal
4. of four
5. class-action
6. *writ of certiorari*
7. concurring
8. rejected
9. judicial implementation
10. judicial restraint

True/False.

1. T	3. T	5. F	7. T	9. F
2. T	4. F	6. F	8. F	10. T

Multiple Choice.

1. c	6. b	11. c	16. c
2. a	7. d	12. c	17. a
3. c	8. c	13. b	18. b
4. d	9. c	14. b	19. c
5. b	10. b	15. a	20. d

Short Essay Answers. An adequate short answer consists of several paragraphs that discuss the concepts addressed by the question. Always demonstrate your knowledge of the ideas by giving examples. The following represent the major ideas that should be included in these short essays.

1. Identify and explain the common law tradition and other major sources of American law.
    *   Common law is a body of judge-made law that originated in England from decisions shaped according to prevailing custom.
    *   The other major sources of American law are federal and state constitutions, statutes, administrative law, and case law.
    *   Constitutions set forth the general organization, powers, and limits of government.
    *   Statutes are laws enacted by any legislative body at federal, state, or local level.
    *   Rules and regulation issued by administration agencies are a source of law.
    *   Case law includes judicial interpretations of all of the above sources of law.

2. Discuss the process the Supreme Court uses to decide cases.
    *   The Supreme Court term begins in October and adjourns usually in June.
    *   The first important decision for the Court is to decide which cases to hear.
    *   Important factors to consider are whether a legal issue has been decided differently by two separate courts and if the Solicitor General is pushing the case.
    *   If the Court decides to hear a case, four justices (Rule of four) must agree to issue a *writ of certiorari*.
    *   Oral arguments will be scheduled before the Court when attorneys representing each side will present their cases.
    *   A private conference will be held in which the justices discuss the case and decide on an opinion.
    *   Opinions can be unanimous, majority, concurring, and dissenting.

3. Describe the presidential appointment process for federal judges.
    *   All federal judges are appointed by the president for life terms, with Senate advice and consent.
    *   The first step in the process is nomination by the president.
    *   Senatorial courtesy can be a big factor in the nomination of federal district judges. A senator of the president's party has a great deal of influence over federal district judge appointments from the senator's state. Senators have less influence over appeals court nominees and no influence on Supreme Court appointment.
    *   Ideology and political party background are two of the most important factors determining who is nominated for federal judgeships.

4. Explain the checks or limitations on the power of the federal courts.
    *   Our judicial system is probably the most independent in the world, but there are important checks on the power of the courts. These checks are the executive, the legislature, the public, and the judiciary itself.
    *   The executive branch has the power of judicial implementation. The way in which court decisions are translated into action is solely the responsibility of the executive branch.
    *   Court rulings can be modified or overturned by lack of appropriations to carry out rulings or overturned by constitutional amendments.
    *   Public opinion is an important factor, since the Court has no enforcement powers; its authority is linked to its stature in the eyes of the public.
    *   Federal judges typically exercise self-restraint in making their decisions. Political questions are issues that a court defers to the decision-making of the executive or legislative branches.

Chapter 14
DOMESTIC AND ECONOMIC POLICY

CHAPTER SUMMARY

The Policymaking Process
The beginning of the policymaking process is the recognition that a problem exists and needs a solution. The Aviation Security Act of 2001 provides a good example of the creation of a policy. There are five basic steps in policymaking:
- agenda building
  The crisis of 9/11 put the issue on the agenda immediately after the attacks.
- agenda formulation
  Members of Congress worked closely with representatives from a number of groups and trade associations, such as the airline industries, pilots, private security contractors, and others.
- agenda adoption
  Congress passed the Aviation Security Act federalizing airport security in 2001.
- agenda implementation
  The major provisions of the law called for airport screening workers to apply to the federal government for employment. New screening equipment will take months or years to install.
- agenda evaluation.
  Evaluation continues, and Congress will receive feedback on the results of the Act.

Health Care Policy
This section discusses the importance of health care policy, the issues of national health insurance, single payer systems, and corporate health insurance. The dilemma for a government in needing to supply health care to citizens coupled with the monetary costs and ideological discussion that this arouses are discussed.

Poverty and Welfare
Historically, poverty has been accepted as inevitable. Industrialized wealthy nations like the United States have been able to eliminate mass poverty through income transfers. An array of welfare programs transfers income from wealthy to poor individuals. The official definition of poverty in the United States is $16,500 yearly income for an urban family of four. The poverty level varies with family size and location. See Figure 14-5 for a look at the official poverty numbers since 1959. In-kind subsidies, such as food stamps, low-income housing, and medical care are not usually counted as income. If these benefits are counted as income, the poverty rate drops. In the wake of the Welfare Reform Act of 1996, the U.S. government provides the following low-income assistance: Temporary Assistance to Needy Families (TANF), Supplemental Security Income (SSI), food stamps, and the earned-income tax credit (EITC) program. The Welfare Reform Act of 1996 gave states more control over welfare programs but also created major new problems for states to solve. The provisions of the law conflict with many state constitution mandates to take care of the needy and require more enforcement provisions that states must pay for. The long-term effects of a loss of income to children in poor families may cause severe problems in the future. Finally, the loss of income may add to the problem of homelessness in the United States.

Crime in the Twenty-first Century
Crime has been a major policy concern since the time of the American Revolution. Two crime issues that have been particularly significant are the rise in violent crimes and the increasing number of serious crimes committed by juveniles. One of the major costs of fighting crime is building new jails and prisons. Illegal drugs are recognized as a major source of crime. Two frequently mentioned methods of solving the drug problem are the get-tough policy of involving major new resources, such as the military, and the legalizing of drugs to take away the economic incentive. A third alternative is to allow states to experiment with these two different approaches. Terrorism has jumped to the top of crime concerns with the attacks on the World Trade Center and the Pentagon on September 11, 2001. Laws have been passed such as the Aviation Security Act, but it is too early to tell if these will be effective on the war on terrorism.

Environmental Policy

The impact of human action on the environment has been a concern in the twentieth century with industrialization and population increases. Federal legislation began in the 1960s to protect the environment. The first major environmental legislation, caused by the Santa Barbara oil spill in 1969, was the National Environmental Policy Act. This act provided for an environmental impact statement (EIS) of major federal actions that might affect the quality of the environment. The Clean Air Act of 1990 addressed the air pollution caused by acid rain. The economic costs have become a significant political issue in the past two decades.

The Politics of Economic Decision Making

Public policymaking is complicated, and nowhere is that more apparent than in economic policy where each policy action carries costs and benefits, known as policy trade-offs. In the world of taxes and subsidies, for every action on the part of government there is a reaction on the part of the affected public. This is known as the action-reaction syndrome. Individuals and corporations facing high taxes will have a big incentive to find or add loopholes to the tax laws. The 2001 legislation to lower the tax rates was undermined by adding new loopholes to the tax laws. The question of taxes in America always raises a discussion of the Social Security tax. The tax on employees and employers is a regressive tax in which people with higher incomes pay lower tax rates than people with lower incomes. The program is basically a pay-as-you-go transfer system in which those who are working pay benefits to those who are retired. The number of people working is declining relative to the number of people retiring, and the large numbers of the baby boom generation will bankrupt the current system when they retire beginning in the early twenty-first century. Numerous proposals to save the Social Security system have focused on allowing individuals to make private investments of social security taxes. No policy decision has been made, but a decision must be made, as nothing can be done to stop the aging of the population.

Changes in taxes are sometimes part of an overall fiscal policy change. A fiscal policy is the use of government spending or taxation to alter the national economy. One approach to fiscal policy is to use government funds to stimulate economic activity in a recession by increasing expenditures and decreasing taxes. Known as Keynesian economics, this policy grew out of the theories of the English economist John Maynard Keynes. Conversely, during inflation, the government should reduce spending and increase taxes to balance the economy.

A monetary policy is also used to alter the economy by controlling the amount of money in circulation, which can affect interest rates, credit, inflation, and employment. Monetary policy works in a similar way to fiscal policy. In times of recession, the economy is stimulated by a greater supply of money and credit. With inflation, the money supply, and hence credit, is reduced to bring down the level of economic activity. The Federal Reserve System, called the Fed and created in 1913, largely carries out monetary policy. The chairperson of the system usually speaks for the entire board. The Fed and its Federal Open Market Committee (FOMC) make decisions about monetary policy eight times a year. Although monetary policy can be implemented much quicker than fiscal policy, it still seems to take over a year to affect the economy. In recent years, the Fed's record has been mixed at best, as some actions seem to have affected the economy in the wrong way.

Politics and Taxation

This section discusses the role of federal income taxes, loopholes, and tax policy.

The Social Security Problem

This section discuses the role of Social Security, its history and functions, and its successes in alleviating poverty among the aged. This section also discusses the politics of altering Social Security and the changes that have been proposed.

World Trade

In this section, the issue of world trade is discussed with reference to the World Trade Organization and protests against globalization.

KEY TERMS

action-reaction syndrome — p. 498
domestic policy — p. 485
earned-income tax credit (EITC) — p. 490
environmental impact statement (EIS) — p. 496
Fiscal policy — p. 503
food stamps — p. 489
income transfer — p. 487

in-kind subsidy — p. 488
monetary policy — p. 503
policy trade-offs — p. 498
public debt — p. 505
Supplemental Security Income (SSI) — p. 489
Temporary Assistance to
    Needy Families (TANF) — p. 489

PRACTICE EXAM
(Answers appear at the end of this chapter.)

Fill-in-the-Blank. Supply the missing word(s) or term(s) to complete the sentence.

1. Courses of action on issues of national importance are called _____ _____.

2. The third step in the policymaking process involves choosing a _____ from among the proposals that have been discussed

3. Social Security is basically a _____ _____ not a pension fund.

4. A traditional solution to poverty has been _____ _____.

5. International trade has become _____ important for the US since the 1950s.

6. A disturbing element of crime in the U.S. is the number of serious crimes committed by _____.

7. The majority of arrests today in the U.S. are for crimes related to _____ _____.

8. The Clean Air Act of 1990 established tighter standards for emissions of _____ _____ and other pollutants.

9. The major environmental law prompted by the Santa Barbara oil spill was the _____ _____ _____ _____.

10. Individuals and corporations facing high taxes will always react by making concerted efforts to get Congress to insert _____ in new tax laws.

True/False. Circle the appropriate letter to indicate if the statement is true or false.

T   F   1. The first step in the policymaking process is getting the issue on the agenda.

T   F   2. Historically throughout the world, poverty has been accepted as inevitable.

T   F   3. The poverty rate today is based on the consumer price index (CPI).

T   F   4. Food stamps are given only to the elderly and disabled.

T   F   5. The problem of homelessness has almost disappeared in the 21st century.

T   F   6. Polls indicate that most Americans are worried about violent crime.

T   F   7. Ozone is the basic ingredient of smog.

T   F   8. The government typically borrows by selling U.S. treasury bonds.

T   F   9. The federal income tax is regressive.

T   F   10. In the past few years, foreigners have come to own about 40% of U.S. debt, while 20 years ago foreign ownership of U.S. public debt was only 15%.

Multiple-Choice. Circle the correct response.

1. The first step in solving a public problem is
   a. to determine the cost involved.
   b. to determine who will be helped and who will be harmed.
   c. for people to become aware of the problem.
   d. for the President to declare a state of emergency.

2. After public policy implementation, the last step is
   a. the variables associated with cost analysis.
   b. policy evaluation.
   c. the ease with which solutions can be accomplished.
   d. policy formulation.

3. A traditional solution to eliminate poverty has been
   a. work programs.
   b. payment vouchers.
   c. education training programs.
   d. Income transfer.

4. The United States has been able to eliminate mass poverty because of
   a. foreign aid from other countries.
   b. sustained economic growth.
   c. in increased work ethic.
   d. mass infusions of tax dollars.

5. The threshold income level for defining poverty was originally based on
   a. the consumer price index.
   b. the cost of a nutritionally adequate food plan by the U.S. Dept. of Agriculture.
   c. guidelines established by the Consumer Protection Agency.
   d. guidelines from the Farmers Union.

6. Policies regulating the amount of money in circulation are part of a
   a. fiscal policy.
   b. national economizing.
   c. monetary policy.
   d. zero sum budgeting

7. The growing number of people claiming Social Security retirements benefits may pose less of a problem than:
   a. Medicare costs.
   b. Welfare costs.
   c. Prison costs.
   d. The trade deficit.

8. A _____ _____ creates free trade among nations, such as the EU or NAFTA.
   a. World trade agreement
   b. Enterprise zone
   c. Free trade zone
   d. Common market

9. The fastest-growing subgroup of the homeless population is
   a. street people.
   b. the mentally ill.
   c. illegal immigrants.
   d. families.

10. The National Environmental Policy Act created the
    a. environmental impact statements.
    b. Clean Air Act.
    c. Ozone limits.
    d. Clean Water Act

11. In recent years, serious crimes committed by _____ significantly increased.
    a. women
    b. juveniles
    c. immigrants
    d. the elderly

12. The majority of arrests today involve
    a. murder.
    b. drug offenses.
    c. federal crimes.
    d. white collar crimes.

13. Legal methods in the tax code for avoiding taxes are referred to as
    a. justifications.
    b. hidden benefits.
    c. loopholes.
    d. give-backs.

14. The United States ran a budget surplus under the presidency of
    a. Ronald Reagan.
    b. Jimmy Carter.
    c. Bill Clinton.
    d. George W. Bush.

15. Monetary policy is primarily made by the
    a. President.
    b. Congress.
    c. Federal Reserve.
    d. Treasury Secretary.

16. Public Debt can be defined as
    a. the limit on how much money Congress can spend.
    b. the yearly amount of money owed by the government.
    c. the total amount of money owed by the government.
    d. the amount of money owed for Wartime expenditures.

17. Opponents of world trade often refer to _____ _____ in developing countries as a reason to oppose globalization.
    a. Trade deficits
    b. Marginalized markets
    c. Social welfare
    d. Slave wages

18. One major reason for the massive increase in U.S. public debt in recent years is
    a. massive increases in social welfare spending.
    b. the war in Iraq.
    c. new prison construction.
    d. tax increases on the rich.

19. The use of fiscal policy to alter economic variables is the underlying premise for
    a. supply and demand.
    b. Keynesian economics.
    c. Marxist economic theory.
    d. the global economy.

20. Monetary policy does not suffer from the same lengthy time lags as fiscal policy does because
    a. monetary policy does not have an immediate effect upon consumers.
    b. the president can act more quickly than Congress to implement monetary policy.
    c. the Federal Reserve can, within a very short time, put its policy into effect.
    d. Congress can act quickly when needed to solve economic problems.

Short Essay Questions. Briefly address the major concepts raised by the following questions.

1. Explain and discuss the steps in the policymaking process.

2. Discuss the major provisions of the Welfare Reform Act of 1996. What impact will this act have on the poor in America?

3. Analyze the issues of crime in the United States.

4. Discuss the major laws attempting to protect the nation's environment.

ANSWERS TO THE PRACTICE EXAM

Fill-in-the-Blank.

1. domestic policy
2. specific policy
3. transfer system
4. income transfers
5. more
6. juveniles
7. drug offenses
8. nitrogen dioxide
9. National Environmental Policy Act
10. loopholes

True/False.

1. T	3. T	5. F	7. T	9. T
2. T	4. F	6. T	8. F	10. F

Multiple-Choice.

1. c	6. c	11. b	16. c
2. b	7. a	12. b	17. d
3. d	8. d	13. c	18. b
4. b	9. d	14. c	19. b
5. b	10. a	15. c	20. c

Short Essay Answers.

1. Explain and discuss the steps in the policy-making process.
*   The policymaking process contains five major steps.
    *   Agenda building is the first step of recognition of a problem. The media, strong personalities, and interest groups usually facilitate this step.
    *   Agenda formulation is the discussion between the government and the public of various proposals to solve the problem.
    *   Agenda adoption is the selection by Congress of a specific strategy from the proposals that were discussed.
    *   Agenda implementation is the government action implemented by bureaucrats, the courts, police, and individual citizens.
    *   Agenda evaluation is groups inside and outside receiving "feedback" about the policy.

2. Discuss the major laws attempting to protect the nation's environment.
    *   Government legislation to control pollution can be traced back before the American Revolution.
    *   The most concerted effort to clean up the environment begins in 1969 with the passage of the National Environmental Policy Act. This law provides for an environmental impact statement (EIS) to be prepared for all major federal actions that may impact the environment.
    *   The 1990 Clean Air Act was designed to clean up air pollution. A major environmental problem of air pollution was acid rain.
    *   The costs of cleaning up the environment have become a major political issue beginning in the 1990s.

3. Identify the difference between fiscal policy and monetary policy.
    *   Fiscal policy is the change in government spending or taxation to alter national economic variables.
    *   Fiscal policy is under the control of Congress and the president.
    *   In a recession, which is a period of rising unemployment, the government will stimulate the economy by increasing government expenditures and by decreasing taxes. During inflation, which is rapid increases in employment and rising prices, the government will "cool off" the economy by reducing expenditures and increasing taxes.
    *   Monetary policy is the change in the amount of money in circulation to alter national economic variables.
    *   Monetary policy is under the control of the Federal Reserve System, or the Fed.
    *   In a recession, the Fed will stimulate the economy by expanding the rate of growth of the money supply. During inflation, the Fed will "cool off" the economy by reducing the rate of growth of the amount of money in circulation.

4. Discuss the issues surrounding the Social Security problem and those of world trade.
    *   Social Security is not a pension fund.
    *   The number of workers per retiree; what it will take to save Social Security.
    *   Controversies surrounding world trade.
    *   Imports and exports.
    *   Free trade and world trade organizations

Chapter 15
FOREIGN AND DEFENSE POLICY

CHAPTER SUMMARY

Facing the World: Foreign and Defense Policy

Foreign policy is a nation's external goals and the techniques and strategies used to achieve them. Two key aspects of foreign policy are national security—the protection of the independence and political integrity of the United States, and diplomacy—the settlement of disputes and conflicts among nations by peaceful methods.

Morality versus Reality in Foreign Policy

From the beginning of the United States, Americans have felt a special destiny to provide moral leadership to the rest of the world. Many of the U.S. foreign policy initiatives seem to be rooted in moral idealism. This philosophy sees all nations as willing to cooperate and agree on moral standards for conduct. The Peace Corps, established by President Kennedy, is a good example of this concept. In opposition to the moral perspective is political realism. This philosophy sees the world as a dangerous place in which each nation strives for survival. The United States has generally pursued a foreign policy that attempts to balance these philosophies.

Challenges in World Politics

In a new development, dissident groups, rebels, and other revolutionaries have used modern weapons to engage in terrorism in order to affect world politics. The long-standing regional conflict in the Middle East has produced a number of terrorist acts worldwide in the last few decades. In 2001, terrorism came to the United States with the attacks on the World Trade Center and Pentagon. President Bush responded to these attacks by military action in Afghanistan, which destroyed Al Queda training camps and brought down the Taliban regime. The dissolution of the Soviet Union brought a lowering of tensions among the nuclear powers, but the number and location of nuclear weapons continues to be a major problem. The emergence of China as a major trading partner of the United States and the most populous nation in the world has altered world trade policies. This is just one of the major developments of the Global economy. Since the 1980s, the United States has become a debtor nation. We owe more to foreigners than foreigners owe to us. Regional conflicts all over the globe have replaced the Cold War as a major focus of U.S. foreign policy. Unrest in the island nations of Haiti and Cuba produced a flood of immigration, which has particularly affected the state of Florida. Conflict in the Middle East between Israel and its Arab neighbors has been a concern of the United States since the conflict began in 1948. In a related mid-east issue, the United States sent more than a half-million troops to push Iraq out of Kuwait in 1991. In 2003, the United States military led a coalition of forces to bring down Saddam Hussein in Iraq. The end of Cold War produced a number of crises in Eastern Europe. The collapse of the former Yugoslavia in Eastern Europe required the intervention of the United States and European nations to prevent the Serbs from killing other ethnic groups. Ethnic violence in Africa also flared in the 1990s. The United States has played little role in these conflicts, except for a limited effort to bring humanitarian aid to Somalia in 1992-1995. In recent years, violence in Africa has been made worse by a wide spread AIDS epidemic.

Who Makes Foreign Policy?

While the President has important foreign policy powers, the Constitution gives Congress the opportunity to review these powers. The two most significant presidential powers are the negotiation of treaties and leadership of the armed forces as commander-in-chief. But Congress has the authority to declare war, and the Senate must ratify treaties by a two-thirds vote. Presidents have used the executive agreements to get around the requirement of Senate-approved treaties. Finally, the Constitution gives the President the right to appoint ambassadors and recognize foreign governments. The president also has informal powers in the foreign policy process. These powers are his access to intelligence from the CIA and military, his ability to influence budget priorities, and his influence on public opinion. In addition to the president, there are at least four foreign policymaking sources within the executive branch. These are:

- the Department of State, the executive agency most directly engaged in day-to-day foreign policy
- the National Security Council, responsible for advising the president on domestic, foreign, and military policies affecting national security

- the intelligence community composed of all government agencies involved in intelligence activities. See page 519 for a list of the most important intelligence agencies.
- the Department of Defense, which brings all military agencies under one organization

Congress Balances the President

The struggle between the president and Congress over foreign policy questions reached a highpoint during the Vietnam War (1964-1975). In 1973, Congress passed, over President's Nixon's veto, the War Powers Resolution. This law required the president to "consult" with Congress before using troops in military action. Congress has also been more cautious in supporting the president where military involvement of American troops is possible. This has restored some of the balance of the relationship of the president and Congress in foreign policy.

Domestic Sources of Foreign Policy

Besides the president and Congress, foreign policy is also influenced by sources in society, which include elite and mass opinion and the military-industrial complex. Public opinion of the attentive public—that portion of the general public that pays attention to foreign policy issues—is particularly important. This segment represents about 10 to 20 percent of all citizens. The military-industrial complex, which President Eisenhower warned the nation about, is the mutually beneficial relationship between the armed forces and defense contractors.

The Major Foreign Policy Themes

An historical review of American foreign policy reveals several major themes. In the early days of our nation, the founding fathers held a basic mistrust of alliances with European nations. The Monroe doctrine of 1823 set forth a U.S. policy of isolationism toward Europe, a policy characterized by abstaining from an active role in international affairs or alliances, particularly with Europe. The end of the isolationist policy started with the Spanish-American War in 1898 and continued through World War I (1914-1918). This policy is generally called interventionism. After World War I, America returned to a policy of isolationism. World War II shattered isolationism forever with the Japanese attack on Pearl Harbor, Hawaii on December 7, 1941. This event ushered in the period of internationalism in American foreign policy that continues today. The United States and the Soviet Union were wartime allies against Adolph Hitler's Germany. After the war, the alliance fell apart, and the United States and the Soviet Union, in a Cold War, began a 50-year struggle for supremacy. The Soviet Union seized Eastern Europe and divided Europe by what Winston Churchill called an "iron curtain." The United States adopted a policy of containment by a series of encircling military alliances to prevent the spread of communist government. The military alliances were tests in a series of military actions, usually by "client" nations of each side. In the Korean War (1950-1953) and the Vietnam War (1964-1975), the United States engaged directly in military action. The Cuban Missile Crisis in 1962 brought the world to the brink of nuclear war, but after this crisis was peacefully negotiated, the United States, and the Soviet Union began a period of relaxed tension called détente. The Strategic Arms Limitation Treaty (SALT) began a process of reducing nuclear weapons. President Reagan's hardstand with the Soviet Union recalled the early days of the Cold War. Reagan's proposal for an expensive, space-based, missile defense system led to the collapse of the Soviet economy and the end of the Cold War. Boris Yeltsin was name president of Russia in 1992 and attempted to lead the nation toward democracy. In 2000, Vladimir Putin was named president and elected to the office in a national election held that year. Putin has supported the War on Terrorism of the United States but did not support the U.S. led invasion of Iraq in 2003.

Foreign and Defense Policy: Why Is It Important Today?

The end of the Cold War has altered the needs of the U.S. military to protect the security of the United States. Regional conflicts will continue to require a more flexible military force. The terrorist attacks on September 11, 2001 emphasized the importance of foreign policy to domestic security. The United States will need to cooperate with organizations like the United Nations to work with other nations to resolve conflicts. The global economy and global issues will become more important to the United States in this century.

KEY TERMS

attentive public — p. 521
cold war — p. 511
containment — p. 524
defense policy — p. 504
détente — p. 525
diplomacy — p. 503
economic aid — p. 503
foreign policy — p. 503
foreign policy process — p. 503
intelligence community — p. 519
iron curtain — p. 524
isolationist foreign policy — p. 523

military-industrial complex — p. 521
Monroe Doctrine — p. 523
moral idealism — p. 504
national security policy — p. 503
negative constituents — p. 519
political realism — p. 504
Soviet bloc — p. 524
Strategic Arms Limitation
   Treaty (SALT I) — p. 526
Truman doctrine — p. 524

PRACTICE EXAM

(Answers appear at the end of this chapter.)

Fill-in-the-Blank. Supply the missing word(s) or term(s) to complete the sentence.

1. _____ _____ describes U.S. goals, techniques, and strategies in the world arena.

2. _____ refers to the peaceful settlement of disputes and conflicts among nations.

3. The _____ _____ is the executive agency most directly engaged in foreign affairs.

4. The _____ _____ formed the basis for the U.S. foreign policy of isolationism.

5. The lasting change in American foreign policy came with the end of _____ _____ _____.

6. The George F. Kennan doctrine, which became the bible of western foreign policy, was _____.

7. President Eisenhower warned the nation about the influence of the _____ _____ _____.

8. The French word that means a relaxation of tensions is _____.

9. The 2005 Iraqi elections were marred by violence perpetrated by _____ insurgents.

10. China sought and was granted _____ _____ _____ _____ for tariffs and trade by the U.S.

True/False. Circle the appropriate letter to indicate if the statement is true or false.

T   F   1. National security policy concerns itself with the defense of the U.S. against actual or potential enemies.

T   F   2. Diplomacy is the set of negotiation techniques by which the U.S. attempts to carry out its foreign policy.

T   F   3. The Peace Corps is a good example of America's moral idealism in practice.

T   F   4. Political realism has always been the only guiding principle in foreign policy decisions for the U.S.

T   F   5. China has become a major trading partner of the United States.

T   F   6.   The State Department's preeminence in foreign policy has gradually increased since WW II.

T   F   7.   The attentive public seems to be less interested in foreign policy than domestic policy.

T   F   8.   U.S. foreign policy during its formative years could be described as interventionist.

T   F   9.   The Star Wars policy of President Clinton brought an end to the Communist threat.

T   F   10. The Truman Doctrine is a clear expression of the U.S. policy of containment.

Multiple-Choice. Circle the correct response.

1. Diplomacy differs from foreign policy in that
   a. diplomacy is a set of techniques and strategies used to achieve a foreign policy goal.
   b. diplomacy is the all-encompassing goal while foreign policy is a sub-set.
   c. the president develops diplomacy and the State Department develops foreign policy.
   d. diplomacy always comes first followed by a specific foreign policy.

2. Foreign policy based on moral imperatives is often unsuccessful for the U.S. because it
   a. makes policy making difficult to understand.
   b. assumes that other nations agree with American views of morality and politics.
   c. requires the president to establish absolute standards of conduct for U.S. personnel.
   d. makes too many enemies.

3. The foreign policy that allows the U.S. to sell weapons to dictators who support American business interests around the world and to repel terrorism with force is the policy of
   a. détente.
   b. moral idealism.
   c. counterintelligence.
   d. political realism.

4. Edwin S. Corwin observed that the Constitution creates an "invitation to struggle" between the president and Congress for control over
   a. economic policy.
   b. appointments to the Supreme Court.
   c. foreign aid.
   d. the foreign policy process.

5. Since the Second World War almost 95% understandings reached between the United States and other nations have come in the form of
   a. protocols.
   b. legislative mandates.
   c. executive agreements.
   d. treaties.

6. The making of foreign policy is often viewed as a presidential prerogative because
   a. as opposed to making domestic policy, most presidents enjoy making foreign policy.
   b. of the president's constitutional power in this area and the resources of the executive branch.
   c. the Constitution clearly denies Congress a role in formulating foreign policy.
   d. the War Powers Act delegated this authority to the president.

7. The major provision of the War Powers Act was to
   a. limit the president's use of troops in military action without congressional approval.
   b. allow the president more freedom in the use of military troops throughout the world.
   c. give the president new powers in the area of foreign policy.
   d. prevent aggressor nations from becoming too strong militarily.

8. Generally, the efforts of the president and the elites to influence foreign policy are most successful with that segment of the population called the
   a. zealots.
   b. mass public.
   c. attentive public.
   d. thoughtful public.

9. The Monroe Doctrine states that the U.S.
   a. had territorial dominion over South America.
   b. was neutral in its relations with Europe and Asia.
   c. could trade openly with China.
   d. would not meddle in European internal affairs and would not accept foreign intervention in the Western Hemisphere.

10. The strategic defense initiative (SDI or Star Wars) was proposed as a program that would deter nuclear war by
    a. shifting the emphasis of defense strategy from offensive to defensive weapons systems.
    b. shifting our defense to an offensive weapons system.
    c. developing more intercontinental ballistic missiles.
    d. allowing for joint United States/Soviet Union development of manned space stations with laser guided missiles for world domination.

11. The event that signified the Soviet Union had relinquished its political and military control over the states of Eastern Europe was the
    a. renewed interest in Cuba.
    b. fall of the Berlin Wall.
    c. defeat in Afghanistan.
    d. dissolution of the Soviet Union.

12. The end of the Cold War means that U.S. foreign policy will need to be
    a. much more stable and predictable than it has been before.
    b. directed at policing the world because the U.S. is the only superpower today.
    c. basically directed at economic aid to underdeveloped countries.
    d. much more flexible in order to deal with changing conditions and complex situations.

13. Operation Desert Storm carried out by the U.S. and a coalition of other nations lead to the
    a. overthrow of Saddam Hussein in Iraq.
    b. overthrow of the Sheikdom of Kuwait.
    c. restoration of the Sheikdom of Kuwait.
    d. overthrow of the government in Iran.

14. More than _____ nuclear warheads are known to be stockpiled worldwide.
    a. 50,000
    b. 32,000
    c. 5,500
    d. 3,200

15. Concern over nuclear weapon proliferation intensified in 1999 when the Senate rejected the
    a. China/North Korea Treaty.
    b. Comprehensive Nuclear Test Ban Treaty.
    c. Middle East Peace Treaty.
    d. Nuclear Terrorism Treaty.

16. Which of the following is NOT an informal technique of the president to influence foreign policy?
    a. his access to information
    b. his ability to influence public opinion
    c. his ability to influence government spending
    d. his ability to recognize foreign governments

17. The role of the National Security Council is to
    a. shape executive agreements for the president.
    b. protect the president overseas.
    c. advise the president on the integration of policies relating to national security.
    d. supervise the CIA.

18. The president who warned the nation of the influence of the military-industrial complex was
    a. Eisenhower.
    b. Nixon.
    c. Reagan.
    d. Clinton.

19. The START treaty
    a. allowed Russia to join NATO.
    b. reduced the number of long-range nuclear weapons.
    c. gave China most-favored-nation status.
    d. created the "Star Wars" initiative.

20. Tensions between the U.S. and Cuba increased tremendously in 1999-2000 because of the
    a. Cuban Missile Crisis.
    b. embargo of Cuba by the U.S.
    c. status of Elian Gonzales.
    d. Cuban takeover of Guantanamo Naval Base.

Short Essay Questions. Briefly address the major concepts raised by the following questions.

1. Describe the formal and informal powers of the president to make foreign policy.

2. Trace the stages of United States foreign policy development from isolationism through détente.

3. Discuss the current foreign policy challenges the U.S. faces today, besides regional conflicts.

4. Summarize the role that the U.S. has played in recent regional conflicts.

ANSWERS TO THE PRACTICE EXAM

Fill-in-the-Blank.

1. Foreign policy
2. Diplomacy
3. State Department
4. Monroe Doctrine
5. World War II
6. containment
7. military-industrial complex
8. détente
9. Sunni
10. most-favored-nation status

True/False.

1. T	3. T	5. T	7. F	9. F
2. T	4. F	6. F	8. F	10. T

Multiple Choice.

1. a	6. b	11. b	16. d
2. b	7. a	12. d	17. c
3. d	8. c	13. c	18. a
4. d	9. d	14. b	19. b
5. c	10. a	15. b	20. c

Short Essay Answers. An adequate short answer consists of several paragraphs that discuss the concepts addressed by the question. Always demonstrate your knowledge of the ideas by giving examples. The following represent the major ideas that should be included in these short essays.

1. Describe the formal and informal powers of the president to make foreign policy.

    *   The Constitution provides the president with two main areas of foreign policy authority:
        *   Article II, Section 1 designates the president as Commander-in-Chief of the armed forces.
        *   Article II, Section 2 gives the president the power to make treaties with the consent of two-thirds of the Senate.
        *   Additional foreign policy power is granted to appoint ambassadors, other public ministers, and consuls. Section 3 gives the president the power to recognize foreign governments.
    *   The informal powers of the president to conduct foreign policy are his superior access to information, his ability to lobby Congress for funds, his influence over public opinion, and his head-of-state moral leadership position to commit the United States to a course of action.

2. Trace the stages of United States foreign policy from isolationism through détente.

    *   The founders of the United States distrusted the European nations and attempted to stay out of European conflicts and politics. This policy of isolation from Europe was stated in the Monroe Doctrine in 1823.
    *   The end of the isolationist policy started with the Spanish-American War in 1898. It continued to change in World War I when the United States intervened in a European conflict.
    *   Isolation returned after World War I in reaction to that conflict.
    *   Isolation ended forever on December 7, 1941, when the Japanese attacked Pearl Harbor, Hawaii, and the United States was thrust into World War II. The era of Internationalism had begun.
    *   Although the United States and the Soviet Union were wartime allies against Nazi Germany, the alliance quickly fell apart after the war. The Soviet Union wanted a divided Germany and seized control of Eastern Europe to create a Soviet Bloc, which would challenge the Western world in an ideological, political, and economic struggle known as the Cold War.
    *   The United States foreign policy throughout the cold War was called "containment" of the spread of Communist nations. This was well stated in the Truman Doctrine: to halt Communist expansion in southeastern Europe.
    *   In the Cuban Missile Crisis of 1962, the United States and the Soviet Union confronted each other over the placement of Soviet missiles in Cuba. This crisis led the world to the brink of a nuclear World War III. After intense negotiations, the crisis was resolved in a peaceful manner.
    *   After the Cuban Missile Crisis, the United States and the Soviet Union realized that they had to reduce the threat of nuclear war. Under the leadership of President Nixon and Henry Kissinger, a period of détente, or relaxation of tensions, began. The first tangible result of détente was the Strategic Arms Limitation Treaty (SALT I) signed in 1972.

3. Discuss the current foreign policy challenges the U.S. faces, besides regional conflicts.
   - Terrorism has become both a domestic and foreign policy problem for the United States. The act of September 11, 2001 has brought terrorism to the United States. Much terrorism has stemmed from the Middle East crisis between Israel and the Arab nations.
   - Nuclear proliferation remains a world problem as more nations join the "Nuclear Club."
   - President Nixon was responsible for opening diplomatic and economic relationships with Communist China in the 1970s. China has become a major trading partner of the United States in the 1990s. China sought and received most-favored-nation status for tariffs and trade policy from the United States. In 1997, China took control of Hong Kong from the British and has preserved the free enterprise system.
   - The global economy has created an interdependent world in which the events of one region can affect the entire world. The political structures of the nation states, perhaps under the United Nations, must adapt and change to deal with the world of the twenty-first century.

4. Summarize the role that the U.S. has played in recent regional conflicts.
   - The island nations of Haiti and Cuba have had a major impact on domestic as well as foreign policy issues for the U.S. Immigrants from both countries flooded into Florida. Continuing problems with the communist government in Cuba led the United States to pass the Helms-Burton Act for an embargo of Cuba.
   - The Middle East crisis between Israel and its Arab neighbors has been a long-standing regional conflict. The United States has repeatedly tried to bring about a peaceful settlement of the conflict.
   - The invasion of Kuwait by Iraq in 1990 has created an additional Middle East crisis for the U.S. In Operation Desert Storm, the United States, with a coalition of nations under United Nations authority, pushed Iraq out of Kuwait. Iraq, under United Nations sanctions, continued to defy the world and created an environment of regional tension. The United States invaded Iraq again in 2003, overthrew the government, and occupies the country in hopes that it will stabilize and be able to run itself as a democracy.
   - The breakup of the Soviet Union leads to profound change in Eastern Europe. The former nation of Yugoslavia broke into a number of nations, which were engulfed in war with Serbia, the dominant part of Yugoslavia. This war continues today, as the United States and other European nations seek a peaceful solution to the conflict.
   - Ethnic conflicts have broken out in a number of African nations. The conflicts have been made more devastating because of drought, AIDS, and famine conditions in many countries. The efforts of the United Nations and United States have been unable to stop the conflicts.